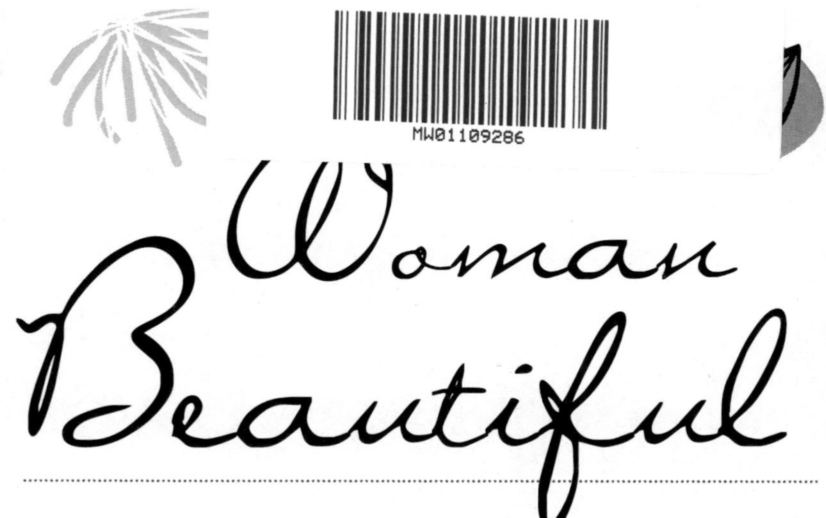

Woman Beautiful

Embracing The Woman God Created You To Be

Amanda Schwab

Tate Publishing & *Enterprises*

Published by Tate Publishing & Enterprises, LLC
127 E. Trade Center Terrace | Mustang, Oklahoma 73064 USA
1.888.361.9473 | www.tatepublishing.com

Tate Publishing is committed to excellence in the publishing industry. The company reflects the philosophy established by the founders, based on Psalm 68:11,
"The Lord gave the word and great was the company of those who published it."

Cover design by Kandi Evans
Interior design by Stephanie Woloszyn

Published in the United States of America

ISBN: 978-1-60696-683-9
1. Religion / Christian Life / Women's Issues
2. Religion / Christian Life / Love & Marriage
09.04.02

For my family, who has patiently loved me, forgiven me, and prodded me on in the holiness of God.

Acknowledgments

I want to say a special *thank you* to:

Jesus, my Savior and Lord; his love has never wavered, and his provision has always been just in time and better than I could have hoped or imagined. Father God, you are all that I need. Your beauty is unbelievable. Thank you! Be glorified.

My husband, John, who prods me on into God's rightness no matter what it takes! I love you, Romey. I wouldn't say that you're beautiful, but you are really cute!

Dr. Richard Tate and the entire Tate Publishing & Enterprises, LLC team; you all are amazingly brilliant. Your knowledge, wisdom, and expertise in the field of publishing blesses and encourages your authors when the rest of the publishing world turns a blind eye. You have enhanced my beauty process in a way that was totally unexpected. Thank you!

My mom, Darlene Eiland, who unbeknownst to her, has shown me how to persevere through the most difficult adversity. Your beauty is eternal. I love you!

My four daughters: Nique, Whitney, Johnette, and Kendra, who grow more everyday in the beauty and joy of the Lord. I love and respect you. You make me so proud. You are women beautiful!

My son, Dallas, who, even though the road has been long and hard, responds to me regularly with the words,

"I love you too, Mom." You are GQ handsome and are reflecting the heart of God more each day. I love you!

My friends, who have prayed for me and blessed me beyond imagining: JuJu Davis, Paula Jackson, Marilyn Salley, and Gwenna Schiffner. You've held my arms up through some very tough years. You're the most beautiful women I know. I love you!

My sister, Teresa Bates, who has shown me that God's best is always worth waiting for, especially when it's not easy. I love you, T! You are more beautiful than words can express.

The many women who have blessed me beyond measure; I hope I've loved you well enough that you know who you are. Your beauty is exceptional!

And to my precious and special friend, my spiritual mentor, Marlene Mains, who speaks bold truth into me on every occasion that we converse. Marlene, you have believed in me, encouraged me, held me accountable, and set me straight. You have prayed for my family and me when I could not. You have taken my hurts, joys, and desires into the throne room of Holy God, knowing and trusting full well in the faithfulness and power of Almighty Father. Without your words of encouragement, and constant reminder of my destiny, *Woman Beautiful* would have been nothing more than a dream slowly fading away, and I would still be struggling in the area of honoring and respecting my husband. Your beauty radiates in every area of your life. I love you, my friend. Thank you!

"Your daily habits determine your future." *Marlene Mains*

Woman Beautiful, what will your daily habits become?

Contents

Foreword

Are you ready to face the truth of who you are and the truth of who you are designed to be? Then welcome to *Woman Beautiful.* As you begin your journey to becoming woman beautiful, prepare yourself as you would any adventure where you will be required to exert some effort and maybe even get a little bit dirty. But instead of physical training, prepare for this journey by opening your mind to the possibility that you have been living life incorrectly. Open your heart to realize where you've been wrong and to learn how to change. Open your eyes to the promise of hope and to see the full beauty of who you are created to be. Finally, open your hands that you can be used to bless others through your beauty.

Through *Woman Beautiful,* Amanda will take you through every aspect of life—mental, emotional, relational, spiritual, physical, financial, and sexual—to challenge you to become completely beautiful. She has filled these pages with personal experiences of which we can all relate and practical applications that allow the light to shine through towards a better understanding of the woman you've been created to be. During your journey to becoming Woman Beautiful, you will find yourself challenging the way you think and what you believe and why you believe what you do.

Amanda is a beautiful woman, wife, and mother who is dedicated to helping all women become beautiful. Yet, she would be the first to tell you that the beautification process is a lifelong journey, and she herself is still living the adventure.

Again, welcome to *Woman Beautiful.* Enjoy the journey. May you never be the same.

Nique Brown

This is a remarkable book written by Amanda as a call from God placed on her heart to help women become who God created them to be. The six aspects of beauty that she effectively communicates will inspire you to begin your own beauty process. Be open, be ready, and be willing to accept the change that God wants to do in you; the rewards will be worth it.

God has placed great value in each of us, and *Woman Beautiful* will help us display the splendor of his magnificent beauty if we will put into practice the truth that we learn on the pages of this book. Amanda successfully lives out these truths every day. I am honored to call her my friend.

Marlene Mains

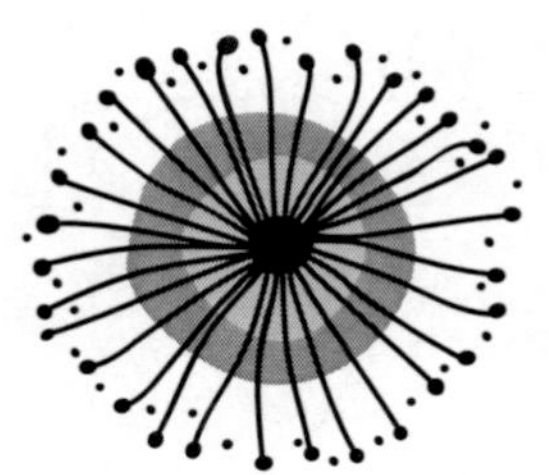

Introduction

Why *Woman Beautiful?* The most important thing I do in a day is love God, my family, and those around me. I realized very early in my adult life that my ability to love unconditionally was feeble at best, being limited by the fallible instruction and love I received while growing up. If I wanted to impact those around me in such a way that it would move mountains and change lives, then I had to rely on the power of Almighty God.

The information contained herein is my personal journey from frail and feeble to fabulous and victorious. God's beauty regimen has proven to be exactly what I've needed to dump the garbage of the past, love selflessly, and deal victoriously with the issues that arise in relationships.

I've listed, in detail, the six aspects of beauty that will aid you in becoming all God created you to be: decorated from the inside out, living and loving in ways you didn't know you could. You'll be freed to be the woman God created you to be while experiencing the joy of a life surrendered to reaching your personal destiny.

The journey you're about to embark on will change your life forever. You are Woman Beautiful!

Praying without ceasing, Amanda

Mental & Emotional Beauty

"She girds herself with strength" (Proverbs 31:17, NAS).

"Strength and dignity are her clothing and she smiles at the future (Proverbs 31:25, NAS).

Some people are thinkers, some people are feelers. When we balance our mental and emotional beauty under the power of the Holy Spirit, God will grow us into a thinker who sincerely feels or into a feeler who can sensibly think. Either is a beautiful blend of God's character.

> "For who has known the mind of the Lord, that he will instruct him? But we have the mind of Christ" (1 Corinthians 2:16, NAS).

Step One

Grow in Like-mindedness with Christ

As a young woman, my days were filled with fulfilling my role as wife, the business of motherhood, and trying to generate extra income for our family. Many of those days brought disappointment and frustration, and I often wondered if what I was doing really mattered. The thoughts that consumed me concerning my marriage and inadequacies as a young mother plagued my mind every day. I didn't realize until many years later just how much time and energy I wasted on inappropriate thoughts. Those thoughts hindered the way I functioned in every aspect of my life. The same ill and impure thoughts can, if they haven't already, invade every area of your life and eventually contaminate and then cripple you. It is vital that you know the truth about your mind and your emotions. The truth is found in God's Word. God loves you; he knows you inside and out. You are Woman Beautiful!

The Mind of Christ—Think with It

The Bible says,

> For though we walk in the flesh, we do not war according to the flesh, for the weapons of our warfare are not of the flesh, but divinely powerful for the destruction of fortresses. We are destroying speculations and every lofty thing raised up against the knowledge of God, and we are taking every thought captive to the obedience of Christ.
>
> 2 Corinthians 10:3–5 (NAS).

Clearly speaking, the battle we fight every day is not physical but spiritual. It is not seen, but unseen. By taking our thoughts captive and making them obedient to Christ's thoughts or truths, we are literally warding off the false accusations brought against us and the haughty overbearing mannerisms of others along with the stronghold they may have on us.

Those false accusations may include such things as: *I'll never be a good wife; I can't even read a recipe. How do I expect to be a good cook? It's my fault that man assaulted me. If I would have been where I was supposed to have been, that*

wouldn't have happened. I will never measure up. No need to try; I'm not good enough, smart enough, or pretty enough. Nobody likes me. There is something wrong with me. What if my husband has an affair? What if I lose a child? The list of lies goes on. They are false accusations Satan will tell you in an effort to destroy your relationships—especially your relationship with God. By whispering those thoughts into your mind through the actions and words of others, he exerts effort to keep you from becoming the Woman Beautiful God intended for you to be. When you replay those thoughts over and over and over in your mind, you become more and more encamped in a stronghold of guilt, shame, fear, and disappointment. And that is not what God has planned for you.

Woman Beautiful, quit believing the lies! Take those tormenting thoughts that keep you captive, and put them under submission and in obedience to Christ. The Bible is clear on who you are and what you are capable of doing and accomplishing under the power of the Holy Spirit. Today is the day that you begin believing new truths about yourself and about him!

Daily Renewal

In order to think with the mind of Christ effectively, it is imperative that Woman Beautiful knows the truths found in God's written word. We are told to "be no longer conformed to this world, *(its way of thinking and acting)* but be renewed by the transforming of our minds, so we can prove *(or know)* what the Lord's will is, that which is good and acceptable and perfect" (Romans 12:2). In knowing scripture, God will reveal so many positive truths about you and him to you that you will be compelled to become the Woman Beautiful he created you to be.

Let me give you a few stark contrasts between the way the world thinks and the way Christ thinks: the world says "Seek to gain: wealth will prosper you," but God says, "Seek Me, I will provide your every need" (Matthew 6:33, NAS); the world says, "Look out for yourself, prosper anyway you can," but the mind of Christ says, "Consider others better than yourself and I will prosper you" (Titus 3:1–6, NAS); the world exploits the young, fatherless, and widows, yet God says "to give special care to these people," (Matthew 19:13–14, Ephesians 6:4, Psalm 82:3, and Ezekiel 22:6–7, NAS). Do you see the difference between the mind of Christ and the mind of the world?

If Woman Beautiful neglects to be constantly renewing her mind, she finds herself caught up in thinking and acting like the world, therefore struggling with her own self-image, relationships, and everyday responsibilities.

Meditating On What's Really True

Meditating on his laws, precepts, and commandments helps Woman Beautiful know God better and understand his promises while enabling her to pull them from memory when needed. God's commands are our guidelines for living the abundant life he has destined for his children. Growing in our knowledge of him promotes love for him, and love for God stimulates the desire to keep his

commands. Or, put another way, love for God stimulates the desire to know his word and to live by it.

It is imperative that you know God's word. To know God's Word is to know the truth! When you know who you are in Christ, you can take every thought captive and therefore break down every lie Satan brings against you. It then becomes possible to entrust to God all that concerns you.

Did you know that Scripture never tells us to just meditate? The Word always says that we are to meditate on the Lord and on his word. When you *just* meditate, you open your mind to whatever fiery dart the devil wants to throw your way. Meditating on the Lord keeps your focus on him, and Satan cannot penetrate a mind set on Christ!

One "meditates" on anything that she willingly gives her thoughts to: hurtful words, frustrating circumstances, difficult relationships, fear over health, money, and an array of life events that are beyond her control. Satan's goal is to keep you meditating on anything and everything but the Lord and his truth.

The word of God says, "You shall know the truth and the truth shall set you free" (John 8:31–32, NAS). By continuing to know the word of God better, more fully, you will experience freedom in the way you view yourself and your circumstances as well as in the way you view and relate with God and others. By meditating on that truth, your mind will be transformed into the like-mindedness of Christ.

My daughter, Nique, once said, "Mom, this is so cool. 'I can do *anything through Christ* who gives me strength'" (Philippians 4:13, NAS) (Nique's emphasis added).

I said, "Yeah."

Nique said, "No, you don't get it. I can go through anything this life might have in store for me because Christ gives me the strength to do it."

I thought to myself, *Wow, what a revelation.*

She, as a teenager, had already begun the process of renewing her mind, meditating on that which is true, and thinking like Christ about this "never too certain" walk of life. I cling to this truth every time a difficult circumstance comes my way. I can go through it victoriously because Christ himself gives me the strength to do so.

My Thoughts, Satan's Doorway

Any open doorway will be used by Satan to keep you entangled in the bondage of fear. God's purpose is to help his children live daily in his saving love. But too often we connect "salvation" with our conversion experience alone. The reality is that God saves us for eternity, but he also saves us every day in difficult circumstances. That is truth! He strengthens us to courageously face challenging people; he affirms us in the midst of heart-wrenching affliction; he holds us in the aftermath of devastating sin; and he lifts us up in disappointment! But if your mind is full of inappropriate thoughts, it is impossible to seek God; therefore it becomes even more difficult to find him in your storm.

Thinking with the mind of Christ is vital to good mental and emotional health. Knowing God's will is key to possessing peace and a sound mind. Understanding who

you are as God's beloved child enables you to set those false accusations at the foot of the cross and live the life God designed just for you. This life includes all of the joy and laughter as well as the hurt and tears you have experienced and will continue to experience. You may not know the reason for some of the trials you go through, but you can know the purpose: to glorify God. Glorifying God should be the heartbeat of every Woman Beautiful.

The best thing you can do in the middle of heart-wrenching and mind-wrecking thoughts is take them captive and turn them to thoughts about the Lord. I like how the Psalmist put it: "When my anxious thoughts multiply within me, your consolations delight my soul" (Psalm 94:19, NAS). Truly, nothing can sooth Woman Beautiful's soul like Jesus. Nothing will close the door that Satan keeps using to dominate your life like meditating on the Lord.

Woman's Emotions

Emotion is defined by Merriam-Webster as a mental state that arises spontaneously rather than through conscious effort and is often accompanied by physiological changes—markedly aroused or agitated in feeling or sensibilities. It is safe to say that all of us have been either aroused or agitated deeply and, really, nobody has to tell us, "Okay, it's time to get emotional." Yet, too often it is our own thoughts (mental) that provoke spontaneous arousal or agitation (emotional). Most of that arousal is unnecessary. I have found in my own life that my thoughts stir up needless worry, fear, and stress within me. Worry, fear, and stress cause a person to become idle, doubtful, untrusting, and suspicious. It also causes one to become lonely, to feel unworthy, and to overreact. Does that sound like some of the anxieties you've been plagued by?

It has been said that women are emotional beings. Praise God! We are created in his image. I am convinced that he is an emotional being; he simply has his emotions under control. It is in knowing whose I am and who I am that I am learning to bring my emotions into check. It is in taking God at his word and accepting Scripture at face value that I can love and be loved without taking more upon my shoulders than need be. God's shoulders are broad, and he can carry my heavy load. It does not matter if it is abuse, neglect, disappointment, or depression; he will carry yours too. God loves you deeply. You are Woman Beautiful!

God Has Deep Concern for You

Isaiah 49:16 is a word picture of hope that we can take hold of as we begin to understand how God views his people. Verse sixteen begins with God saying, "Behold, I have inscribed you on the palms of my hands," and ends with, "Your walls are constantly before me." God's love for his people is so intense that he has written their names on the palms of his hands. I remember when God first gave me revelation of this verse. My mind's eye saw Jesus holding out his nail-scarred hands. I was immediately reminded of the sacrificial love that he has bestowed upon me and

the many others who have given their lives to Christ. My name, your name, has been written on his hands in such a way that it cannot be removed.

The "walls" God talks about in this verse are the walls that surrounded the city of Jerusalem. Those walls kept out the wicked who were bent on destroying God's people, and within those walls lay everything that concerned his people. Even though the walls of Jerusalem lie in ruins, God reminded his people that their brokenness was constantly before him and he would rebuild their walls. Your walls may be lying in ruins all around you—through death, divorce, or perhaps by your own making—but when God says your walls are continually before him, rest assured that all that concerns you is continually on his heart and mind. He will be faithful to build them back up in such a way that blesses you and glorifies him.

Perhaps you're in a time of peace and prosperity. Give thanks to God! Your walls are still constantly before him. Or you might be feeling as if you're in a state of unbearable and irreparable destruction. Remember, all that concerns you concerns him. You, your family, ministry, health, home, career, happiness, holiness—all of you is always on his heart and mind. He has your best interest at heart continually. Shout hallelujah!

Fear Instigates Worry

There was a time in my life that fear dominated my world. I worried over everything. As a child, it was things such as a possible WWIII or perhaps a divorce between my parents.

As a teenager, it was self-worth and rejection. And as an adult, it was fear of losing a child, or my husband having an affair. These are just a few of the many fears that I had. But to God be the glory—he used fear to get my attention, and by his grace he gave me victory over fear, and now I am more than a conqueror! (See Romans 8:35–37.)

Are there times when I experience fear? Yes, but now that fear is fleeting. It is only by his grace and goodness that I can keep my fear in check. I have learned to recognize when I am experiencing fear because I worry or am troubled in my spirit, and I ask God to show me what it is that concerns me. He faithfully reveals the exact fear issue, and I can then pray through that fear, trusting him to take care of whatever it is that has me in the bondage of worry.

Fear takes many forms: fear of being rejected; fear of not being loved; fear of not getting one's desires; fear of loss of money, job, health, or loved ones; fear of not measuring up; fear of not getting your way; fear of having to live somebody else's dreams; fear of the past; and the list goes on.

As long as you are living in fear, you will be an emotional basket case! As long as you are living in fear, you *will be* an emotional basket case. Do I need to say that again?

If you will submit your fearful thoughts to Christ and make them obedient to his plan for your life, you can take them captive and live daily in a state of peace and trust.

My Heart, God's Business

As the psalmist wrote poems, prayers, and songs out of his personal life, two certain truths became very clear to him: God knew him inside and out, and he loved him deeply. Psalm 139:23–24 expresses the psalmist's desire to know what God already knew: "Search me, O God, and know my heart; test me and know my anxious thoughts. See if there is any hurtful (offensive) or wicked way in me, and lead me in your everlasting way" (my paraphrase). The passionate desire of the psalmist was to know himself in such a way that necessary changes could be made in him, in order that, by the power of the Holy Spirit, he would be led in the way of God's everlasting *righteousness.*

Anxious thoughts and offensive ways can be your own inappropriate or sinful attitude and behavior directed toward another person or your best kept secret(s), such as sexual, physical, emotional, or spiritual abuse you've endured. Harboring secrets that torment you and keep you in a state of hurt or fear are secrets that need to be dealt with. Sometimes those secrets include horrific treatment to you by others or even by you toward others. Those issues need to be dealt with no matter how painful they may be.

There is more fear and hurt in living with a memory than in confronting the past and dealing with it. I'll say it again. *There is more fear and hurt in living with a memory than in confronting the past and dealing with it.* Joyce Meyer puts it well. She says, "There's going to be pain either way. Why not choose healing?" Joyce is talking about the sweet healing and wholeness that only comes through working through the difficult issues and mindsets that have plagued many women for what has turned into years, even decades.

Anxious thoughts reoccur until issues and fears are finally acknowledged and dealt with. Woman Beautiful, don't delay one more day. Seek the healing relief that comes by working through those difficult hurts that have instigated fear in you for so long.

When the psalmist sought revelation on his offensive ways, it was because he wanted to bring glory to God. He knew full well that offending others was a character defect that could be changed. This holds true today. So much of the way we treat others stems from the image we hold of ourselves. If we can get God's eye-view of ourselves, it becomes easier to love others, even like others, and therefore we will be less likely to offend those around us or to be offended by them.

How do you view yourself? Don't describe the physical you. How do you value yourself? Do you know how deeply God loves you? Are you convinced that he created you out of love for you and a desire to fellowship with you? Do you believe that he always has your best interest at heart? Do you know that he has destined you to do something that no one else can do because it has been especially designed for you alone to accomplish? Can you look in the mirror and say, "I am valued by God and he loves me just the way I am?" Have you ever heard the statement, "I'm somebody cuz God don't make no junk?" No matter what you've been through, God places immeasurable value on your life and his purpose for you.

You, Woman Beautiful, are precious to him. He created you *beautifully and uniquely*. You are loved *with an*

everlasting love. You have been *destined for a great purpose. Every part of you is valuable to God. You are a child of God*—that is everything, and everything is enough! (See Psalm 139:14, Jeremiah 31:3, Jeremiah 29:11, 1 Thessalonians 5:9, Matthew 10:31, Romans 8:16–17, 1 John 3:1, and Hebrews 13:5.)

What about Depression?

Biologically imbalanced depression is very real and must be treated by a professional physician. By biological, I mean depression that naturally occurs because of one's biological structure. Most depression, however, is not of that nature but is self-induced and can be successfully overcome.

This depression is what I call "I syndrome": *What about me? When do I get what I want? He always gets what he wants. Why doesn't anybody call me to go have a soda pop or cup of coffee? My life has been so hard. So many bad things have happened to me. Nothing I ever do turns out the way I want it to. When will it be my turn?* When one's life becomes all about herself, it will usher in a state of depression. Every thought consumed with self is one step deeper into depression, and it will refuse to go away until Woman Beautiful gets her heart and mind set on something other than herself.

I have yet to talk with anyone suffering from depression, that is, who is not biologically depressed, and whose first words don't begin with "I" and end with "me." And I am convinced that, because of varying reasons, depression runs high among the Christian community: we do not self-medicate by way of drugs that have not been prescribed, excessive alcohol, illicit or impure sex, and other stimulants; we are too ashamed to get counseling, but most importantly, we neglect to turn to the one who says, "I, the Lord, am your healer" (Exodus 15:26, NAS).

My friend Marlene openly admits that she was once an active member of the "Pity Party Club." In fact, she was president. But, realizing the destruction that being self-absorbed brought to her life, she quit the club and began a life of being others-centered.

Woman Beautiful, it is vital to your mental and emotional well-being that you know God's identity and willfully become God-centered. In knowing who God is and by focusing our attention on him, we are able to know who we are.

God is not an insignificant *anybody* that we can just do whatever we want or a bothersome *nobody* that we can ignore, contrary to what many people believe—including some who claim to be Christian. He is holy, awesome, Almighty God with the power to avenge and to bless (Isaiah 5); the one who fashioned you into his likeness (Genesis 2:22, Genesis 1:27); the Creator and Sustainer of the universe and everything in it (Genesis 1:1, Psalm 55:22, Psalm 71:6, Genesis 1:14, Psalm 104:9); the One who spoke all that you see into existence (Genesis 1:1–31); the God who has loved you at your most unlovable state (Romans 5:8); quick to love and slow to anger (Psalm 86:15, Psalm 103:8); the Forgiver of all your sins (Psalm 130:4, Acts 10:43, Ephesians 1:7); the One True God who sent his only son to die for you (John 3:16) and, he alone is worthy of your

praise and adoration (Revelation 4:11). So, whatever praise Woman Beautiful can muster up, we need to shout it unto him because it is due his good name, and praise for him will cause depression to lift!

God has done so much for us by way of his goodness. We are truly indebted to him, in the form of praise, for eternity. As Juanita Bynum put it, "If God never did another thing for me, it would take me a thousand years to give him the praise that's already due his name." He is Holy God: perfect and pure in thought and deed, the one who loves, accepts, encourages, delivers, believes in, enjoys, dances over, and delights in you. Therefore, we as believers are to take on his identity because he is worthy of imitating and because he has loved us so well. We take on this new identity by focusing on the one who knows us best. The only one who is worthy of being imitated—Jesus Christ. It is through him that emotional health and healing can be achieved, by contentedly trusting God in whatever circumstance you might find yourself in.

Even though the life you are now living may not be the ride you stood in line for, you can still have good mental and emotional health. If Woman Beautiful will change her focus, she will change her emotional health. Claim the promise of Isaiah 26:3, which states that the person whose mind is set on the Lord, he will keep in perfect peace, because he trusts God. Peace, beloved Woman Beautiful, is God's desire for your life; trust him wholly and let God work out *his plan* for you.

God in heaven, I praise your holy name. I ask that my every thought would be consumed with you. Lord, reveal any anxious thoughts that I have to me, and enable me to surrender those thoughts to you. Father, I don't want to be controlled by my emotions any longer. I know that my fears only instigate worry. In that worry, I doubt your concerned involvement in my life. Lord, forgive my doubt, the unbelief that prevents me from basking in the truth of your unwavering, selfless love which has been poured out on me and all that concerns me through Jesus Christ. Lord, I trust you and believe that you have my best interest at heart at all times. When fear tries to consume my thoughts, remind me to take those thoughts captive and make them submissive unto you. Teach me to be others-centered beginning with you. Stir up praise for you in my heart and mind whenever I start to focus on myself and the adversity I face daily. Father, I trust you! Thank you for your faithfulness to me. I love you, Lord. In Jesus' name. Amen.

Beauty Tips

1. Practice saying, "Satan, get thee behind me! My thoughts belong to the Lord."
2. Look in the mirror and say, "I am a pillar and supporter of God's TRUTH!"
3. Remind yourself of these truths everyday:
   - I am a child of the Most High God. (Galatians 4:1–7)
   - I was created for God's divine purpose. (Jeremiah 29:11)
   - I am the head and not the tail, I am above and not beneath. (Deuteronomy 28:13)

- To God I am the fragrance of Christ. (2 Corinthians 2:15)
- I am fearfully and wonderfully made; a wonderful work of God. (Psalm 139:14)
- All I do prospers because I walk not in the counsel of the ungodly, I stand not in the pathway of sinners, I sit not in the seat of the scornful. God's law (word) is my delight and I meditate on it day and night. I am a tree planted beside streams of *Living Water.* I bear fruit in season and my leaves do not wither. (Psalm 1:1–3)
- No weapon formed against me *or my household* shall prosper and every tongue which rises against me in judgment, God will condemn. This is my heritage from the Lord and he will vindicate me. (Isaiah 54:17)

4. Memorize 2 Corinthians 10:5
5. Ask the Holy Spirit to search you, revealing to you what you need to know about yourself right now.
6. Thank God in your present suffering and for the glorious blessing you are getting in position for.
7. Make your life an expression of gladness. Confess victory and be glad because your hope rests in Christ alone and he is faithful to do what he says he will do. Hallelujah!
8. Identify one thing that keeps you going back to being fearful. Take it before the Lord asking him to reveal all that it entails to you - then you can pray through it, trusting him to deliver you from the bondage of fear.

9. Memorize Philippians 4:13
10. Say to the Lord, "I trust You Lord." Tell him again, "I trust You Lord." Tell him again and again and again, "*I trust you Lord!*"

Relational Beauty

The heart of her husband trusts her, he will have no lack of gain (Proverbs 31:11)

She rises while it is still dark and prepares food for her family, even her servants (Proverbs 31:15)

She extends her helping hand to the poor (Proverbs 31:20)

Her husband is known in the community (Proverbs 31:23)

She opens her mouth in wisdom and the teaching of kindness is on her tongue (Proverbs 31:26, NAS)

She takes good care of her family (Proverbs 31:27)

Step Two

Become Others-centered

Woman: fashioned by God in the likeness of God. What a beautiful picture. She was divinely designed to engage in relationships first and foremost with God, then with her husband, children, other women, and men who are not her husband.

Relationships make Woman Beautiful tick. Those relationships rich with the qualities of trust, acceptance, approval, and value move her into a mode of willful change and betterment. She desires to become all that God created her to be, and she knows that this change is better and different than she is today. With the right heart-attitude and mindset she will far exceed anything man has expected and even demanded that she try to be.

Relating to Her Husband

Taken from Man

God created Adam because he wanted fellowship and communion with someone like him. He wanted to be loved, needed, and honored. From the beginning, God has desired to have an intimate relationship with man. As rewarding as that relationship was for God, he knew it was not good for the man to be alone.

Woman's purpose for being created was for the man. Even though Adam had God and walked and talked intimately with him every day, he knew that Adam needed a companion that he could commune with and that would help him. So God put Adam to sleep, removed a rib from his side, and from that rib fashioned Eve—the first woman. I find it interesting that the King James translation of the Bible calls Eve his helpmeet rather than a helpmate. She was created to "help meet" Adam's needs (Genesis 2:18). Woman Beautiful has not been called to fill God's spot in her husband's heart; she has been given to him to fill a spot God *would not fill:* that of sexual intimacy, procreation, face to face physical interaction, and physical help. God had all he wanted in Adam, but Adam did not have all he needed in God. Does that sound like your husband? Next to Christ, the relationship we share with our husbands should be the most important and the most rewarding in our lives.

Respecting Him

In her book, *The Power of Femininity: Rediscovering the Art of Being a Woman,* Michelle McKinney Hammond explains how man was created in God's image, therefore man wants what God wants. God wants worship and honor. Man wants the equivalent: respect. Too many of us are so busy being offended by our husbands—and for some rightfully so, that it seems impossible to walk in an attitude of respect toward them. Yet, Woman Beautiful's husband deserves respect for two reasons: because God created him, and because she is told to respect him in the book of Ephesians, the Bible.

Proverbs 14:1 says, "The wise woman builds her house but the foolish tears it down with her own hands." I played the role of the foolish woman, tearing my house down with my very own hands. Every time I allowed myself to be offended by John, I withdrew my love from him, consequently showing him little to no respect. I didn't realize the damage I was doing. Unknowingly, I brought a full-blown assault on my marriage and home.

It took me a very long time to look at my husband with respect and honor. The hurt he seemed to inflict came so frequently, I felt as if I were constantly forgiving him and trying to start fresh in our marriage. I gave him lash after lash in my thoughts and spent countless hours in an attitude of "withdrawn love." I finally came to realize that every day I chose to linger in hurt, disappointment, and frustration constituted nothing more than the truth of Proverbs 14:1. For many years, I was that foolish woman: being wounded by John's carelessly spoken words, becoming bent out of shape by his inability to understand me, and experiencing frustration due to the way he interacted with our children; all of which caused me to withdraw my love. I now choose not to be offended and am therefore better able to maintain my love and respect for him. Please don't misunderstand, there are times that John and I both say and do things that are borderline idiotic, but we are learning how to manage those times with love and forgiveness and with an attitude of understanding.

There is a big difference between respectful love and

Eros love. You can respect your husband (or the men in your life) without having deep feelings of sexual-type love for him. Erotic love is the added blessing for a woman in marriage. (You will understand that better in the Sexual Beauty segment of this book.) Men and women both long for that wild, "in love," passionate feeling. Once experienced in marriage, it seems to be the ultimate expression of love in the husband and wife relationship. But, for many women, Eros love lasts only for a brief time in the beginning of marriage. With the first major hurt, wild love heads for the door and woman spends many of the next several years trying to recapture that sensual loving feeling.

That "loving feeling" is a form of respect toward him. In fact, sex comes in second so closely to respect that he will sometimes get the two confused. We women think, *If you loved me, you would know how I feel,* but man thinks, *If you respected me, you would want to have sex with me.* Woman Beautiful, you cannot respect him and refuse to have sex with him. (Unless there is a physical reason why you can't have sex.) Respect without sex sends an accurate message of, *My wife does not respect me.*

To show him honor and respect in both private and public conversation does more for his manhood than just about anything else a woman can do for a man. Words are powerful. The word of God says, "and God said, 'Let there be light,' and there was light," (Genesis 1:3, NAS). God literally spoke the universe into existence. Proverbs 10:20 says, "The tongue of the righteous is as choice silver, the heart of the wicked is worth little." Proverbs 15:4 says, "A soothing tongue is a tree of life, but perversion in it crushes the spirit." And Proverbs 18:21 says, "Death and life are in the power of the tongue, and those who love it will eat its fruit." Your words about and toward your husband have the power to make him or completely break him. Just as God's words were powerful to create an entire universe and civilization, so are your words powerful to assist God in building a good and godly man. Woman Beautiful, you need to get a revelation about your words. They are powerful! Life and death exist in your words. Do you speak life, or do you speak death? Is your husband steadily growing and maturing, or is he slowly dying a very painful death?

If you don't know how to honor him with respect, then ask him for some ideas. As I said previously, the way we speak to him and about him in public expresses respect or the lack thereof; the way we interact with him in front of our children tells him at what level we respect his God-given authority over our families; offering some bedroom fellowship, when he's had a stressful day says, *You're important to me* and heeding his instruction screams loud and clear, I might add, *I value and trust you.* When he shares those ideas with you, be sure to implement them. Part of your purpose as woman is to help him grow into the likeness of Christ, therefore becoming the man God created him to be. If your man is not becoming what God intended him to be, then perhaps you are not doing your part. Your part begins with respecting him, and respect is an attitude that shines through in the most difficult of circumstances.

One Flesh

Because so many men classify the act of sex as complete oneness, this area of marriage demands more discipline and work than just showing respect. Not that you would come into agreement with him claiming that the sexual encounter is the ultimate in oneness but that you would wait patiently on God while he convinces your husband that it is not.

Women have, for a long time, understood the oneness concept, and our oneness connection far surpasses a twenty-minute rendezvous once or twice a week. We have not successfully conveyed our understanding to our husbands; nonetheless, we know that true oneness far exceeds any kind of physical encounter we may share with the man we love. Don't get me wrong, the sexual relationship is vital and evidence of a healthy and thriving marriage, but the marriage can be healthy and thriving no matter how often sex takes place. For women, oneness takes place when there is genuine love, respect, and honor in a marriage. True oneness is the fruit of a loving and kind relationship where the other person's best interest maintains a permanent "first place" in the heart.

A woman who has a healthy oneness relationship with her husband rests securely in his love. She trusts his judgment and knows that she and her children take top priority. They stand second only to Jesus Christ. Her every concern is of great importance to him. She doesn't feel used by him sexually because he is so connected to her daily. Sexual intimacy is a natural response to a day well-lived and a relationship well-cherished and managed.

The word of God says, "and the man and his wife were both naked and were not ashamed" (Genesis 2:25). There will be many things in marriage Woman Beautiful finds difficult to share with her husband. Yet, honesty plays a major role in oneness.

In the beginning of marriage, it could very easily be her physical nakedness that brings some shame, but a woman quickly gets over that. More difficult to share without shame could quite possibly be her childhood, an unhealthy or illicit relationship, something she's done, or, in my case, financial debt. No matter what her "shame" issue might be, Woman Beautiful must take it before the Lord and ask him for the strength and courage she needs to share it with her husband.

There may be certain things God does not want disclosed to her husband, such as an affair. It is written that we are to, "Confess our sins (to God) and He will be faithful to forgive us our sins and to cleanse us of all unrighteous" (1 John 1:9, NAS) (my interpretation added). It also says, "Confess your sins one to another and pray for one another that you may be healed, *the heartfelt prayer* of a righteous *(wo)*man accomplishes much" (James 5:16, NAS) (my emphasis added). Sometimes Woman Beautiful has to consider what will be in the best interest of the other person. If her "shame" issue is of the magnitude that it could bring death to her marriage, she will definitely want to seek good spiritual counsel and pray fervently before she reveals such a painful and damaging truth. Without exception, honesty, trust, forgiveness, and acceptance are the most important attributes needed in achieving the oneness God intended in the husband/wife relationship. Keep in mind, prayer has to precede all issues, and prayer coupled with godly counsel has to precede some issues. Such issues could include past or present behavior, such as addictions, sexual conduct, or perhaps unbridled spending. Other issues may include the gross misconduct of others that directly involved you: sexual abuse, theft, random violence, or maybe, abortion.

Submit. Do I Have To?

To submit in rebellion is not submission. Let's quit thinking it is!

I used to think that submitting in anger or resentment was better than not submitting at all. Then God revealed to me the truth about my submission: it was done in an attitude of rebellion, and the reality was it only made for a bad witness and bore the fruit of problems rather than blessing. Wow! I might as well have not been submitting at all. Please don't mince my words. You and I have been called; yes, told, to submit to our husbands. Not if he is kind, loving, and compassionate. Not if he gives you everything you want. Not if he tries to understand you. Not if he comes home on time every evening, and not if he never forgets an important date, but to "submit to him just as if we were submitting unto Christ" (Ephesians 5:22).

As difficult as it was, Christ submitted out of reverence toward God. In the garden of Gethsemane, Christ fell to his knees and cried out, "Father if there be any other way (to save these people) then take this cup (of suffering) from

me, but Father Your will be done not mine" (Matthew 26:39, NAS) (my emphasis added). Christ would have preferred a different way of completing God's plan of salvation, but more than that, he wanted to bring glory to his Father. He knew this glory would come only through complete obedience and submission. Jesus could have backed out of the plan, but he wanted to honor his Father, God. So in complete willful submission, he endured brutal beatings, relentless ridicule, being spat upon, and mocked. He did not hold back: wearing a crown of thorns and being nailed to a wooden cross. He eventually gave his own life over to death (Matthew 27), and if that were not enough, he went to the very pits of hell and did our prison time (1 Peter 3:18–19). Woman Beautiful, you and I are to submit to our husbands out of respect for them and obedience to God no matter how difficult it may be.

I distinctly remember the ten minutes worth of marriage counseling John and I received immediately after our wedding rehearsal:

"John, what do you think 'to submit' means?"

"If I move to Liberal, Kansas, she has to go with me."

"That's right. Amanda, what do you think submission means?"

"I have to do what he tells me to do?"

"That's right."

If I could do things over, the most important things I would change are summed up in the way I submitted to John in the early years. Being "told" what to do is the last thing I bargained for in marriage. But, submitting is so much more than heeding someone's command. Submitting is continuing to listen when you would rather tune him out; trusting the Lord when your husband's instruction doesn't seem to make sense, and praying through while pressing on when you would rather bow your back, dig your heels in and fight to the finish. Submitting is not always getting your way, and it is certainly not having the last word. To submit is to humble yourself before God and your husband—even if he is displaying behavior that is immature, self-serving, or manipulative.

You have been called to be your husband's mate–of equal value; as his mate, you are to speak the truth and then leave the outcome to the head authority. I'm not telling you to be silent; I'm encouraging you to submit.

Submission Is an Act of the Will. It Is a Heart Attitude.

It's not your job to change your husband. You have been called to respect him and to speak the truth to him in love. It is God's job to do the changing. Do you hear what I am saying? God is the one responsible for changing your husband. You just do your part of respectfully loving him and submitting to him, and watch God work.

For those of you who have had to bear ridicule for your faith in Christ, for those of you who have had to take your children to church alone for many years, and for those of you who have quietly served God desiring to be more active in your church, rejoice and give thanks; the hard walk we have had to endure here on earth will be the closest any of us as born-again believers will ever come to hell.

For the many who have endured harsh verbal abuse, watched your children be beaten down by words of anger and suffered unnecessary pain involving the people, ideas, things, and dreams you covet: be faithful. Do not grow tired of doing what is right and what is good; your reward will be great! So, shout praises to the Lord, and submit to your husband as if you were submitting to Holy God.

Let me say this, submitting involves speaking the tough words that need to be said. During one of our counseling sessions, I had to ask John if I could "ask him questions until I understood what I was to submit to." Although that is difficult at times, it always brings clarification and unity. It may not be unity that I would have preferred, but it is unity nonetheless.

Divorce. What about It?

The truth of the divorce matter is that God hates it. Malachi 2:16 says, "'For I hate divorce,' says the Lord, the God of Israel, 'and him who covers his garment with wrong,' says the Lord of hosts, 'So take heed to your spirit, that you do not deal treacherously'" (NAS). God was talking to the Israelite men. They had been treating their wives and families treacherously, and it grieved God deeply. Because he placed such high value on the covenant between him and the man and woman at the beginning of time, he hates divorce. It is the most violent or treacherous attack a (wo)man can make against their own family and ultimately against themselves and God.

Have you ever considered divorce? I would dare to

say that most of us have. We seem to think that perhaps divorce would be better than the situation we're in. That, Woman Beautiful, is a lie straight from hell. Don't believe it and quit considering it! The Bible says that Satan "is out to kill, steal, and destroy" (John 10:10). The first thing he will do is go to work on your marriage. Do not give him the victory. Scripture says, "Greater is He (the Holy Spirit) who is in you than he (Satan) who is in the world" (1 John 3:3, NAS) (my words added). Woman Beautiful, you have an advocate, Jesus, who constantly sits before the Father, petitioning him on your behalf (1 John 2:1). He will not give up on your marriage; don't you give up either.

Because man's heart was hardened and he would not do what God commanded him to do, what God created him to do, or what God expected him to do, Moses had to provide a means of divorce (Mark 10:5–9). God, therefore, gave Moses a set of rules by which a man could divorce his wife. Yet, under the new covenant, Jesus gave only one reason for divorce: infidelity, or more powerfully stated, sexual immorality (Matthew 5:32). For a husband and wife to divorce for any other reason was unacceptable to God. The covenant made between him and the husband and wife is a covenant to be honored until death alone separates the two. When God says, "My grace is sufficient," (2 Corinthians 12:9) a woman can trust that his grace will be all she needs to remain steadfast in a difficult marriage.

Abuse? Abandonment?

There is a vast difference between a difficult relationship and physical abuse. God does not intend for any Woman Beautiful to stay in a physically abusive situation. I cannot counsel her in any direction other than this: she must protect herself and her children. Sometimes, the only way for complete and permanent protection is through complete and permanent separation.

Please notice that I did not include verbal abuse; it falls in the category of "difficult marriage." God can, will, and does help those who suffer verbal abuse. He helps those who are stayed on him overcome the mental and emotional dysfunction and pain caused by verbal abuse. Stand, focused on him, and he will give you beauty for the ashes that others have harshly heaped on you.

There is one other reason for divorce that many will argue is acceptable by God. That is the reason of desertion; if a husband leaves a wife, then she can go through with a divorce. I stand in agreement with this but before Woman Beautiful runs to the attorney's office, she needs to *pray.* God may be doing a work of sanctification in her husband that he couldn't do while the two were living together. I know it sounds crazy, but Jesus gave Peter over to Satan to be sifted for a while and when he came back to the Lord he was a man equipped to strengthen his fellow believers (Luke 22:31–32). Seek the Lord. Trust the Lord. He will not lead you astray. He is not a god of confusion. If you seem to be confused, get counseling from a reputable Christian counselor. But beware, just because "Christian" is in one's title or business name does not mean that the counseling service is reputable. Do your homework; check his or her references, and try to find a few people who have had restorative success with a particular counselor.

Remember, God hates divorce and he considers it treacherous dealing. The definition of treacherous is providing insecure footing or support; marked by hidden dangers, hazards or perils; characterized by faithlessness or readiness to betray trust; deceptive, untrustworthy, or unreliable.

God knows the devastating damage divorce causes a person and a family. To tear a marriage apart with divorce not only tears apart a family, but it tears the heart of God. When a couple unites in holy covenant with God, they become a "cord of three stands that cannot easily be broken" (Ecclesiastes 4:12, NAS). If a couple divorces, they make him part of their heart-wrenching sin. This treacherous treatment toward a wife or husband and their children brings a curse of insecure footing, hidden dangers, distrust, and deception on the entire family. It becomes very difficult to trust anyone, including God.

When Woman Beautiful divorces for any reason other than unfaithfulness, she curses her own family. Her treatment is treacherous toward her husband and children. She cannot divorce and be whole. One cannot be divided by one in marriage; the end result is two halves. God is loving and kind. He is patient and joyful. His desire is to bless and not curse. He wants to and will rebuild the marriage of a woman whose heart and mind is stayed on him.

The Consequence of Divorce

There is a high price to pay for divorcing. That price is "single-hood." For some, that would be a seemingly welcome state, but for others, impossible. Divorce because of infidelity is acceptable to God, but biblically one is instructed to remain single. Though Paul implores any person who cannot control *her* own lusts to marry rather than to sin against God by fornication, he also makes it clear that being single is a gift from God. The Bible minces no words; remarriage after divorce for any reason is sin against God, the new marriage partner, and against oneself. Not only that, remarriage comes with its own suitcase full of problems.

Near the end of my first marriage to a practicing alcoholic who was verbally, physically, and sexually abusive, and who indulged in one affair after the other, God very lovingly and patiently began nursing me to health. But at that time, I was a twenty-three-year-old single mom of two beautiful little girls, and the last thing I wanted to do was spend the rest of my life without a mate. During my daily prayer time, I would petition the Lord without failing for a man to love and be loved by and to share my life with. One morning, while on my knees crying before God, he very compassionately said, "Amanda, if you will let me, I will be your companion." That was independence day for me. I got up off of my knees, wiped away the tears, and never asked God for a man again. Two months later, I met John.

Because I didn't know the word of God well enough at that time, he allowed me to marry John. In fact, I believe he brought John to me for the purpose of marriage. I say *brought him to me* because God is a god of love, tenderness, and blessing. He delights in making beauty of our ashes, cleaning up our messes, and showing himself as strong and sufficient in our turmoil. When I determined in my heart that God was enough, he honored my request for a mate.

I would like to say our marriage started out blissful and stayed that way, but it did not. Through much perseverance, two things have continued to grow: our love for one another and my absolute dependence on God. Yet, even with our love for each other and God's unwavering help, I continually struggled with the hurtful words that John seemed to so easily hurl at our children and me. (Woman Beautiful, please don't think that I had nothing to do with John's behavior. I bore severe lack in the way I respected John and in the way I expressed love to him. Coupled with both of our dysfunctional backgrounds, we were a mess.) God would have preferred that I stayed single, but in his infinite knowledge and wisdom, he brought me a man that he loved more than I could ever love; not because John was such a bad person, but because God loves so purely, completely, and unconditionally.

Though it may seem as if divorce would be the better remedy, which also is a lie from Satan. The best scenario is an intact family: Dad, Mom, and children living wholly in one house. The wounds of daily life can be helped and healed through consistent prayer and steadfast love. In knowing the word of God, Woman Beautiful can effectively help herself and her children through faith and encouragement and by resting assured that God's promise

stands firm: "All things (will/do) work together for the good of those who love God and are called according to His purpose" (Romans 8:28, NAS) (my words added). My children, husband, and I love the Lord, and I know that we have been called according to his purpose. As hard as divorce is and as hurtful as marriage can be, I trust that God has used and continues to use our trials to grow us more into the likeness of Christ. We are and will continue to tell the world of God's faithfulness and of his praiseworthy deeds.

As I contemplated divorce many times over the first seventeen years of my and John's marriage, I would have done my family a much better service had I learned to look at my husband through the eyes of Christ in the early years. But the deeper the pain, the more frequent the thoughts of divorce.

When I began asking the Lord to let me see John the way he sees him, then my attitude began to change toward him. I saw a man who was mortally wounded and in need of unconditional love and acceptance, who needed to be valued and respected. I saw a man who was loved greatly by God and whom Jesus Christ died for. I began to realize that his need for control was a cover-up for fear; fear of being treated disrespectfully, abusively, and unjustly, just as he had been treated as a child and teenage boy. I saw a man whom I could not love the way he needed to be loved apart from a complete attitude change; that, Woman Beautiful, would take an act of God. If our marriage was to be a successful one—not just a marriage that existed in the realm of hurt, fear, and disappointment—then I had no choice but to let God do his good work in me. I remember my friend and spiritual mentor saying to me on one occasion, "Well, if God doesn't change him or take him out, then what are you going to do?" By the time of this conversation, I had finally come to grips with divorce and knew that it was no option. Her question forced me to confess out loud what I would do if God brought no change to John's heart and mind. My response was, "I'm going to continue to pray, do what I know to do as a godly wife and mother, and speak the truth to him in love."

Speaking the truth in love is more difficult than it sounds, especially for someone like me. I have the keen ability to be "in your face" honest, and it doesn't always come across as loving concern for the person I'm talking to. But because I've always been concerned with hurting a person's feelings, I choose my words carefully and can usually convey what needs to be said without crunching her spirit unless I have direct hurt involved.

Speaking the truth in love becomes a whole different story when Woman Beautiful is experiencing emotional hurt. It is probably safe to say that about all of us Woman Beautifuls. The truth of the matter is truth does offend. Jesus himself never offended anyone with anything other than truth. So rest assured, no matter how a person speaks it, truth will be offensive. That's why speaking truth in the right heart attitude becomes so important. By changing the word "love" to "kindness" it becomes easier to speak to the person who's offended you. The word of God says, "For He Himself (God) is kind to ungrateful and evil men" (Luke 6:35, NAS) (my words added). When we are kind

to people who seem to have intentionally hurt us, that kindness is on loan to God, not the person. He will pay it back with great reward. God does not let our Christ-like behavior go unnoticed. He is faithful to honor us if we are faithful to honor him in the way we treat those who seem to be our "enemies." Woman Beautiful, kindness toward your husband will bless your children, and it will promote healing in both you and your husband as well as in your marriage.

Who's Leaving? Not Me! I'm Cleaving!

The word of God says, "For this reason a man shall leave his father and mother and cleave to his wife ..." (Genesis 2:24, NAS). I heard someone once say, "A daughter is a daughter for life, but a son is a son until he takes him a wife." If your husband has not yet cut the umbilical cord, then you have the painstaking chore of prayerfully helping him cut that cord. I say painstaking because, as you already know, a mother's hold on her son seems to be made of titanium. The breaking away that should have started in very early childhood is not only many years behind but by now is very deeply rooted. As difficult as it will be, your marriage depends on it. Bathe your husband and your in-laws in prayer. Ask a praying friend to pray with you during this breaking away process that you and the Lord will be taking your husband through. The ride will not be nearly as bumpy if you will maintain an attitude of kindness both toward your husband and his parents, especially his momma.

Even though the Bible tells man to cleave to his wife, the wife has her own cleaving to do. For women, it is somewhat easier to leave and cleave. Woman Beautiful finds much of her identity in her husband; therefore, the tie between the woman and her parents can usually be severed with little effort. In fact, the severing of ties usually means a new level of relationship between Woman Beautiful and her parents. This new level should be a relationship of encouragement, continued training, and assurance.

Our daughter, Whitney, married under unfavorable circumstances. Her marriage had tremendous adversity stacked against it in the beginning. John and I knew our part in her marriage was to help her be the wife God created her to be no matter what. There were times when it would have been easier to counsel her to leave the relationship. But the greater joy has been to confidently counsel her to honor her husband and trust the Lord. I can remember telling her many times over, "Sugar baby, honor your husband and God will honor you. If you will honor your husband, God will honor you." Woman Beautiful, the Lord wants you to honor your husband and he will be faithful to honor you.

Cleave to your man and trust God to grow your marriage into the one flesh relationship he intends for you. If either you or your husband refuses to cleave to one another, your marriage will be built on shaky ground, and it will never become what God planned for it to be.

Don't think that leaving one's father and mother is the only "leaving" a person needs to do. Woman Beautiful has to leave her own selfish desires in order to cleave wholly.

Her husband has to do the same, but it is not her place to insist that he let go of self-centered ambitions. Her role is to speak the truth in kindness, and then let God take care of the rest. Remember, you too have cleaving as well as leaving to do. Your marriage goal is not to be one-sided but to become one-fleshed.

Saved, Unsaved

There is a very old dilemma many Woman Beautifuls struggle with when it comes to her husband's salvation: is he saved or is he not? We live in such a time that it is quite difficult to tell who is truly Christian and who is not. By Christian, I mean a sincere and committed follower of Christ Jesus. Many claim to be Christian, but few know that the term "Christian" literally means to *be a studious follower of Christ who will, after time, look like a little Christ:* learning to think as he thinks and to respond as he responds; to love as he loves and to be totally committed to Yahweh, the one true God, just as Christ is committed to him.

The struggle between judging and not judging has rendered many of us confused in determining whether or not our mates are Christian. Far too often, the behavior and words of our husbands leave us as a heap of undetermined identity—both our identities and theirs. When a decision seems to be anything but God-centered or a behavior leaves one hurt, confused, belittled, or humiliated the question enters our minds: "Is this man really a Christian?" That, beloved Woman Beautiful, is *not* for you to be concerned with. If your husband claims to be Christian, then you treat him as he claims.

For many years, I struggled with my husband's claim to Christianity. That struggle kept me guessing on just how exactly to relate to him. One day, he would be loving, generous, kind, involved in church, and striving toward spiritual maturity. The next day, he would be nasty, mean, ugly, and would want nothing to do with God or anything concerning him. I struggled with how to pray for him, how to speak to him, how to love him, and how to encourage him. You name it, I struggled with it.

Only in the past few years have I finally determined in my head that, *John says he is Christian; that is how I will treat him.* If the Lord tells me to say a certain something to him, then I say it. If I am instructed to speak Scripture to him, then I speak it. When God says, "Tell him I said!" then I tell him. This has not been an easy act of obedience. Many of you know exactly what I'm talking about. With the help of my spiritual mentor, Marlene, who reminds me to walk like it's so, talk like it's so, act like it's so, and think like it's so, I am experiencing greater victory in treating John like the Christian man he claims to be—every day.

As I have said, "Treat him as he claims." You can, as a Christian woman, expect your Christian husband to act as a born-again believer. If he responds in any way other than as a loving and godly man, then it is your God-given responsibility to "help him" reach the high calling God has placed on his life: the high calling of holiness. (Now, before you get too excited, he gets to "help you" meet your high calling, which is also holiness or what I like to call inner beauty.)

The word of God says, "As iron sharpens iron, so does one man sharpen another" (Proverbs 27:17). You and your husband have been given to one another to sharpen one another with grace, love, and forgiveness. And you have been implored to, on every occasion, "speak the truth in love (kindness), so that he (and thee) will grow up in all aspects into Him who is the head, even Christ" (Ephesians 4:15, NAS) (my words added). Once a person "claims" to be Christian, then it is Woman Beautiful's awesome opportunity to help that person grow up in Christ Jesus, especially if it is her husband.

I heard Dr. Charles Stanley put this truth in a powerful way recently: "God gave you your husband to help take him to the place he could not have gone without you. And he gave you to your husband to help take you to the place you could have never gone without him." Wow! What a freeing way of looking at your husband.

It is time to quit being tossed back and forth. Today is the day to keep pushing on in the power of Holy God. Let him take you both where you could have never gone without him. Almighty God entrusted you with your husband to help him become the man God created him to be. Stop and consider this: God wants to take you and your husband to places you could have never gone without each other.

Father, thank you for my husband. As difficult as it is at times, I am so grateful to you for entrusting me with him. Lord, teach me to love him unconditionally and without expectations. Let me see him through your eyes. Enable me to love and encourage him, to forgive him daily, and to prod him on into the righteousness of Jesus. Enable me to express respect for him to him. Convince him that honoring him is my top priority. Grow us into a married couple that glorifies you in every area of our relationship. Delight in us as we delight in you. In Jesus' name I pray. Amen.

Relating to Children

> "Her children rise up and bless her" (Proverbs 31:28, NAS).

Who Has Perfect Children?

Before you go thinking that my family is picture perfect, please think again. Over the years, I've had children involved in drugs and alcohol. I've visited a child in jail and at drug rehab. I've been called obscenities, cursed, and given the infamous instructions on where I could go and what I could do to myself while there. I've been called a liar, two-faced, and holier-than-thou. I've done diversion with two children, and I've had three children leave home on bad terms. We've had to deal with premarital sex and the effects thereof, and on many occasions I've heard my children quote Scripture only in an effort to throw it in my face. Right now I'm wondering why I'm writing this book. Yet, the Lord reminds me that I write in an effort to help you be the best Woman Beautiful mom you can be.

Most of us have had the opportunity to rear our children to adulthood, I realize; though many women have lost children or aborted children, given children up

for adoption, or even have children who have walked away from them. Whether your children are there in your home, in heaven, being raised by another woman, or somewhere across the country, they are your children nonetheless. Praying for them and thanking God for them is vital to you and to them. Also, there are women who have no children and will never have children. You, dear Woman Beautiful, have the opportunity to touch and change the lives of kids whom nobody else will. In each circumstance, you still have a relationship with them. Although it may be one-sided right now, you can still do your part.

I believe we would all agree that our children are our most prized gifts from God. They are our greatest joys and some of our deepest sorrows. They make us laugh when we feel like crying, and they cause us to cry when we'd rather be laughing. Yes, there are times when we wonder what we were thinking when we decided to have kids, especially when they're between the ages of about eleven and sixteen, but still they encourage us and motivate us to become the best that we can be.

God's Plan, Not Mine!

The plan I envisioned for my children was one of teenagers who actively loved their parents and the Lord—kids who wanted to do right in the eyes of the Lord and who earnestly sought him. I hoped my children would hate the ways of the world and choose to serve God wholly. My plan included spouses that loved the Lord with their whole heart and loved my children selflessly. I've prayed fervently for many years that the Lord would lead us into a family ministry where we would serve our Savior together, bringing glory to him. More than anything, I've prayed that my children would be totally sold out to Jesus Christ. I clearly remember asking the Lord to allow my children to go through whatever it would take for them to surrender their lives completely to him. He told me that some of them would have to go through much hurt: the pain of hitting rock bottom before they would surrender fully to him.

As difficult as it's been to watch my children hurt, it's been even more exciting to be reminded of God's faithfulness. Many years ago, the Lord gave me revelation of his love for my kids. That love far surpasses any amount or depth of love I will ever have for them. His love is more protective, more powerful, and more productive than mine could ever be. And God's plan for their lives makes my plan for them look pointless.

It took me a long time to let go of the plan I had for my children. But once I did, the most amazing changes began taking place in me. My trust in the Lord concerning my children started growing, and tough love became an effective tool not so much in my children but in my own mind and emotions. I stopped taking things personally and was able to simply love my kids. If a child became so angry with me that they lashed out with hurtful words, I was able to keep on loving that child and even remain hopeful in God's promise to complete the good work in her/him which he alone started. My peace began to be less and less interrupted, and my joy quit flying out of the window. It has become so much easier

to love my kids unconditionally and to keep from harboring hard feelings toward any of them.

I am convinced that the struggle they encounter every day between the world and its influences and holy God and his purpose for their lives is powerfully difficult. My job is not to become angry because of this struggle, but to compassionately love each of my children and to encourage them in the ways of the Lord. I am to implement discipline when it is needed and love on every occasion. I know it's easier said than done at times, but loving discipline should always be the goal, and tough love—authority executed in a love arena—is vital to every healthy parent-child relationship.

It's time that parents stop battling with their children over the influences of the world and begin loving them through this brief and extremely difficult walk on earth. By letting go of unrealistic hopes and dreams for our kids, we release God to love them through us and work out his plan for them. He will give them their own dreams and their own plans, and *if* we will be faithful to pray for them, teach them God's word, and direct their eyes and hearts toward him, he will bring forth a plan that is custom-designed just for them. And beloved Woman Beautiful, God's plan will blow a momma away!

Jesse's plan for his youngest son, David, was to be nothing more than a shepherd boy, but God had a different plan. Hallelujah! David was very young when God privately anointed him king. It was many years later that David was publicly put into office. The years between his anointing and his actual taking office were years in which God used to prepare David for the task. It does not matter how young or old or strong or weak your children may be. It may appear as though your children are not actively seeking the Lord. What becomes most painful to a Woman Beautiful mom is what appears to be deliberate defiance toward parents and the Lord in both the hearts and attitudes of her children. But things are not as they appear; he still has a plan for each of them. It is your sweet obligation and divine privilege to lead them in his way, no matter how difficult that leading may be!

Which Way Should He Go?

I've come to understand that at the birth of each of our children, we as parents enter into an eighteen-year training period with them. We begin a process of training them to live life as adults in a way that is beneficial to others, profitable for themselves, and most importantly, glorifying to God. Scripture says that we are to "train up our children in the way they should go and when they are old they will not depart" (Proverbs 22:6). Some people say that this verse means that "we are to train our children up in their natural bent." I strongly disagree with that statement. In my opinion, they have misinterpreted this verse. Perhaps they have confused talents and gifts with God's righteousness. These are clearly two different aspects. The word of God says that our natural bent (natural man) is the way of sin. God hates sin. So we certainly better not let our children go that way. We indeed are to train them up in the way of the Lord. This is the only way they should go. If we train

them up in his way, then we can believe that even when they are old they will not depart from it. Shout hallelujah!

Surely we are to help develop their talents and gifts, but most importantly, we are to lead them into God's righteousness by training them up in his way, which is the only right way. Helping our children know God *is* training them in the way they should go.

Knowing God, not just who he is, becomes the most challenging yet, most profitable, teaching and training we do. In knowing him, our children will know and understand his purpose for their lives, his promises, his provision, his peace, and most importantly, his personality or character. It should be our goal as godly parents to teach our children the way(s) of Holy God so that they will be prepared for the greatest challenge of all: adulthood. In order to train them in the way they should go, we must be willing to teach and train with not only our words but also by our lives. In doing this, we have no choice but to embrace this challenge ourselves: by training ourselves under the influence of the Holy Spirit in the right way(s) of God. Perhaps the word could also say, *Train up a parent in the way she should go and when she is old she will have trained up Godly children.*

God's Heritage

The Bible tells us that children are the Lord's heritage. As his heritage, parents have the responsibility to help their children know the Lord. This teaching and learning process comes by speaking the word of God to them, talking openly and honestly with them about the expectations of the Lord, and by constantly reminding them that they are loved greatly by him. More importantly, it is living a godly life before them. Yet, too many times, a person puts so much concern on the past that one can't see the rich heritage that God has given them in the present.

It's the past that keeps a person from living in the now. We serve a now God, and he fully expects parents to teach their children how to love and live both with and in the now of God. God's name for himself is "I AM." Not I was or I will be, but I AM. One of the best things Woman Beautiful can do for her children is to let go of her parents' methods of child rearing and take hold of the word of God and teach his truths to her own children. God's instruction on life is infallible. And when he calls our children unto himself, whether at a very early age or in later years, we are obligated to him to surrender them to him and his purpose for their lives.

If your parents did something good while rearing you up, then take that and run with it, making it better than even they did. But if your parents did some things very poorly, then throw those as far away from you as the east is from the west. Do not repeat that same dysfunctional behavior.

You do not have to become like your parents, doing things as they did; you can become like me (Jesus), doing things as I do. This is one of the most freeing truths Christ has taught me as I've been rearing children. Too often we believe that rearing up children the way we were reared is the only right way to do it. Sadly, all of us grew up in homes with

fallible parents. Once I took hold of who my children really belonged to, God, and who I was created to reflect, him, it became a personal mission to rear them up under God's instruction and not necessarily that of my parents.

My children, whom I know are really not my own, are seen by God as beautiful and precious. They can be called "the apple of His eye" (Psalm 17:8). Jesus himself said, "Let the little children alone, and do not hinder them from coming to me; for the kingdom of heaven belongs to such as these" (Matthew 19:14, NAS). Children are loved greatly by God, and he places a very high value on them. This verse clearly identifies two things: children are never too young to be called by God to himself, and, we as parents and even church leaders need to get out of his way!

When my daughter, Johnette, was seven years old, she led one of the little neighbor girls to Jesus. She and Susie came running in all excited about what had just happened. I encouraged Susie to go home and tell her mother what she had done. (I felt sure she would be thrilled that her daughter had invited Christ into her life.) The two came back to our home shortly thereafter and were both broken in spirit. Susie's momma told her she was too young to understand what she had prayed and that nothing really happened. The excitement of Jesus and his love was short-lived because momma got in the way of what God was doing in her child's life. Woman Beautiful, God speaks every language and every age level. He communicates with your child as an infant better than you will ever communicate with him or her as an adult. Get out of his way.

God's Heritage, God's Workmanship

God has a purpose and a plan for each of your children. Because children are his rich heritage, he needs to be able to shape them and mold them according to his desires. If Woman Beautiful constantly bails her kids out of difficult circumstances, covers up their mistakes, enables them to be irresponsible, protects them from an insensitive dad, or cushions their lives in such a way that their own hard knocks feel like nothing more than a small bump in the road, God will never be able to do in her kids what he wants to do. I know the word of God says that God's plans will not be thwarted, but an interfering mom can certainly cause more stress and strain in the maturing process than need be. Remember, all of what I write about is my personal experience. Love must be tough, not mean,—tough; there is a big difference. When you step out of God's way and let him do in your children what he wants to do, you will be practicing tough love.

Simple Kindness

Because we are training up God's heritage, we have the responsibility to do this training in a godly manner. If I can describe God in one word, he is *love.* If I can describe love in one word, it is *kindness.* Everybody responds to kindness. If we as Woman Beautifuls expect to grow up godly children in the midst of impatience, hollering, negativism, and accusations, then we have believed our own lie. The children we raise up will be impatient,

negative yellers who accuse others of everything, including their own wrong behavior. These kids will also suffer from poor self-esteem, a sense of sure failure, and an inability to love others well. It is God's personality growing in us as godly women that enables us to assist him in developing his character in them. The word of God says, "A gentle answer turns away wrath, but a word harshly spoken stirs up anger" (Proverbs 15:1, NAS), and King David implored his servants, "For my sake do not deal harshly with the young man Absalom" (2 Samuel 18:5, NAS). I believe this is exactly what God says to us: *For my sake, do not deal harshly with the young children.* When we act kindly toward (our) children, we reveal God's goodness to them for his own sake. We exemplify his character to our children, and that in turn can create in them a desire to know him better. Woman Beautiful's kindness toward her children is an expression of God's love and concern for them.

I didn't say, *Spoil them.* I didn't say, *Give them everything they want.* I didn't say, *Don't discipline them.* No, I said, "Train up yourself in the way you should go and when you are old you will have reared up disciplined, well-balanced, godly children who love the Lord." And from that, they will not depart! Holy God will take great pleasure in his heritage.

Things Are Not as They Appear

It appeared as though Abraham and Sarah were too old to have children; it appeared as though the children of Israel met a dead end at the Red Sea; it appeared as though Esther would have lost her life for going before the king uninvited; it appeared as though Daniel was to be eaten by a den of lions; and it appeared as though Jesus was dead and buried. But, things are not as they appear! Hallelujah! Though it may not look like it, God *is* working in your children and on behalf of your children. Confess his faithfulness and remind yourself daily that he is the one who promised to "complete the good work in *your kids* that He *alone* started" (Philippians 1:6) (my words added). No matter what it may look like now, things are not as they appear!

What You Confess Is What You Possess

For many years, I confessed laziness, rebellion, disobedience, and other such negative traits about my children. I was ignorant in the truth of God's word that says, "In the tongue is the power of life and death" (Proverbs 18:21, NAS). It didn't occur to me until my children were almost all grown adults that I had been speaking a form of death on them with every negative word out of my mouth: death of dreams, desires, and goals; death of esteem, identity, and purpose; death of relationships both with me and their dad, but mostly with God.

More powerful than anything else you do for your children are the words that you continually speak to them, whether they be positive, life-giving words or negative, death-bringing words. When I finally began to change my confessing, God went to work in my children but, more than anything, he went to work in me.

Some of our daughters struggle with their weight.

I distinctly remember God telling me to tell one of our daughters that she is beautiful every time I see her eating other than at meal time. In obedience, I've begun speaking God's truths of her beauty both on this daughter and into her heart. I don't know what it does for my girl, but it's doing an amazing work in me. I'm reminded of just how beautiful she is both inside and outside. She has a beautiful, generous heart and is very caring for others as well as God's creation. She is a great joy to be around, and her beauty is constantly developing. I am confident that the beauty she radiates will one day penetrate the hearts and minds of the people she has opportunity to minister to.

What, Woman Beautiful, are you confessing about your children? Do you tell them they are lazy, ungrateful, or irresponsible? Do you point out their disobedience and rebellion? Change your speech about and toward your children as needed and watch the good work that God does in both you and your kids.

O Lord my God, I often wonder why you chose me to mother these beautiful kids. The love you have expressed to me through them blows me away. Lord, forgive the times that I have spoken harshly to them, the times I have acted insensitively toward them; forgive my cross words that have wounded their spirits.

Father, love my children through me in such a way that they would long for you; therefore, pressing on in their relationship with you.

Lord, you are a beautiful example of the loving and compassionate parent that I long to be. Grow me into your likeness and be glorified through me. In Christ's name I pray. Amen.

Relating to Other Women

"She opens her mouth in wisdom and the teachings of kindness are on her tongue" (Proverbs 31:26, NAS).

God "fashioned" woman into the feminine of himself. Now that is a noteworthy statement! Have you ever considered the fact that God is a beautiful balance of masculine and feminine? Men are his masculine side and women are his feminine side. If you've ever wondered why God can be all things to both genders, it is because he is the single mold from which we were both taken.

Genesis 2:22 says, "The Lord God fashioned into a woman the rib which He had taken from the man, and brought her to the man." Merriam Webster says the word "fashion" means "to give shape or form to; to train or influence into a particular state or character." God gave woman the shape and form of physical beauty and then trained her and influenced her into the likeness of his gentle and emotional characteristics. I've often wondered about the perfection of man, woman, and all of creation before the fall of man; that is, before sin entered the picture. I can see Eve in all of her beauty and grace, laughing playfully with Adam without a care in the world. She was a picture of purity, beauty, and perfection. I don't think beauty has been so amazingly displayed in woman since Eve.

She and Adam were both flawless: physically, mentally, emotionally, spiritually, relationally, and sexually. Although they were created to live forever, one thing would eventually stand between them and God: their ability to choose. Choosing to disobey was certainly their downfall.

At that exact moment, sin entered the world and they both became very aware of their nakedness. Shame came upon them and the inner beauty and grace that Eve possessed, enabling her to be in good relationship with both God and Adam, took a flying leap. Woman Beautiful has been striving for that balance of grace and beauty coupled with purity ever since.

One of the most important relationships we find ourselves struggling with is the relationship we share with other women. We *need* each other yet, so many of our relationships never graduate past the acquaintance level. Many factors enter into the reason we have few intimate friends.

Friendship

Friendship is the one thing women desire from other women above everything else. The relationship that includes two close friends is a peculiar thing. I've come to understand that the friendships that God orchestrates are the ones that last forever. I've never been one to go looking for friends. I've just lived life, letting God bring those women to me whom he wants my life to cross paths with. Let me explain.

My friend JuJu, is a strong woman of God who thinks before she speaks and diligently seeks out ways to glorify him. After seeing her a few times at church and Mothers of Preschoolers (MOPS), a support group for mothers of preschool aged children, we had a divine, accidental meeting in front of the dairy case at our local grocery store.

Unbeknownst to me, her two-year-old child had been sexually assaulted by a teenage boy at our church, and JuJu needed someone to talk to. It was the common ground of Jesus Christ and mutual sensitivity to the Holy Spirit that she and I share that opened the door for a lifelong friendship in front of the butter and sour cream that day in 1990.

Through her deep need to share the hurt she was experiencing and my need for a friend, God brought two broken pots together, and we have enjoyed each other's company ever since. Our physical relationship has dwindled to having lunch together a couple of times a year yet, when a prayer need arises we both know who to call.

Paula is the most vivacious woman of God anyone will ever meet. The book on "cool" was written about Paula. Even though our circle of friends was totally different, we had a mutual attraction toward one another that seemed would never be acknowledged, that is until one day at MOPS. I happened to be working with the Moppetts, the young children of the MOPS attendees, that Friday morning when Paula came be-bopping in with her usual bubbly self. What she said to me not only caused me to evaluate my life but, started a friendship that would last forever. Her words went something like this: "I woke up at five o'clock this morning and couldn't go back to sleep, and well, God told me I needed to spend time with you." Woman Beautiful, I can't tell you the strength and courage that must have taken Paula. My friend has come from a background of neglect, abandonment, and sexual abuse. It took total dependence on the Lord in order for Paula to obey the leadership of the Holy Spirit that morning. You see, it was another one of those divine accidental meetings; it was only the evening before that I had been asked to work with the MOPS children. Paula had no idea that I would be there, and I'm sure she thought she would have a little bit of time to think about what the Lord had said to her. I was delighted; God was giving me a really cool friend and she was getting a friend who would love her and accept her just the way she was.

As time went on, Paula and I found a ton of things that we had in common: our chewing gum of choice is Wrigley's Double Mint, the thought of a tomato sandwich causes us both to salivate, Vienna sausage right out of the can is a fun treat, we love our husbands in much the same way, and we can find a positive in every difficult situation. The list goes on, but you get the picture. The most powerful few things we have in common, though, is the once long-held fear of rejection and our burning desire to know God better, love him more, and to be pleasing to him. Thankfully, God, by his infinite grace, steadily delivers us from the fear of rejection and, though we are far from perfect, he continually calls both Paula and me unto himself to show us how to love him more, know him better, and bring glory to his holy name. Paula now lives in the Kansas City area, but miles cannot prevent a friendship that God initiates; we pick up right where we left off every time we converse.

Marilyn is a cut above the rest. The day she rang my telephone is a day I will never forget. Marilyn and I had a mutual friend who had recently moved to Topeka. Our friend had given my name to Marilyn and asked her to pray about contacting me. He told me I needed a friend with a like spirit, and he thought Marilyn would be just the woman. I remember thinking, *Yeah, whatever.* I didn't know Marilyn, but was sure she had more important things to do than try to connect with me. So when my phone rang and it was Marilyn Salley, I was totally surprised. She said she was compelled by the Holy Spirit to call me. You could hear in her voice that making this phone call was an act of obedience and not desire. She invited me to participate in a women's Bible study her church would be starting soon. I did, and the rest is history.

Marilyn is the kind of friend whom you can look in the face and neither one of you has to say a word; there's just a mutual compassion and understanding for one another. Marilyn has prayed for me and encouraged me in some of my deepest times of hurt. She has never passed judgment on me, even when I've had to explain some "not so acceptable" ideas to her. Some of the those ideas include such changes as giving up coffee and Pepsi—my pop of choice, and replacing it with an occasional glass of wine at meal time, or filing for a divorce, when we all know God hates divorce. She has simply said, "Even though it doesn't make sense, I know you've heard the voice of the Lord and you need to do what he says." Her belief in me has catapulted me to the next level. Marilyn too has moved; she now lives seven hours away in the Tulsa area, yet I look forward to every opportunity we have to sit face-to-face and converse as kindred spirits.

The friendship Gwenna, my faithful Monday morning

prayer partner, and I share just kind of fell into place. I don't remember exactly how our friendship started, but I am convinced it began with prayer. She and I enjoy each other's company and bask in the sheer pleasure of some of the smaller things of life: the color lime green, flowers, old stuff, and children, especially grandchildren!

Gwenna grieves deeply over the state of the church and our country. She hurts when other people hurt, and she laughs when others laugh. Gwenna is the kind of Woman Beautiful that pours out her heart to God on behalf of someone else's need. Her love for the Lord flourishes and her burning desire to see his will being done surpasses her own hopes and dreams. Gwenna is faithful to pray because she knows prayer moves the mighty hand of God. If you're looking for either of us on Monday between 11:00 a.m. and noon, you'll find us at the altar, prostrate before God, petitioning him on behalf of the church, our country, our friends, and our families.

Marlene is almost indescribable. She is a funny and bold visionary. Her knowledge of the word of God never ceases to amaze me. Her spiritual understanding and interpretation of the Word is fresh and freeing. She speaks the truth and is intolerant of God's people behaving godlessly. Marlene is quick to admit her own shortcomings and grieves deeply when God reveals her sin to her.

We met through our mutual friend Marilyn Salley. Marilyn had invited us to her church for their monthly women's fellowship. I was amazed by Marlene's sensitivity to the Holy Spirit and her eagerness to share a word from God with whomever he might have a message. Even though our relationship was at an acquaintance level only, that was about to change.

Marlene's husband of nearly twenty-six years was diagnosed with cancer in early February of 2004. Marlene buried her beloved Harold on February 26th of that same month and year and that, Woman Beautiful, put Marlene in an immediate position of need—namely the need for work. My husband and I had been talking and decided it would be okay for me to hire someone to come in once a week and help me do those things a busy wife and mom seems to rarely get to: mopping, scrubbing toilets, wiping out window seals—you know what I mean. Marilyn suggested I contact Marlene. So in early April of 2004, Marlene came to my house in the form of an answered prayer, ready to clean. A true godsend, little did I know I was not only getting house help but also a spiritual mentor.

On the second Thursday she came to clean, Marlene showed up with tears flowing. She repeatedly said, "It's all about the change." Remember, Marlene and I had only been acquaintances, and when she talked about "the change" I thought she must be going through menopause. But by the beginning of May, I knew the change Marlene was going through had nothing to do with the physical and everything to do with the spiritual. Her desire to grow more into the likeness of Christ surpassed every other area of her life, every desire she possessed, and every dream she once had. Losing her husband would not be a place of bondage, but an opened door for change. Marlene decided she would not walk the road of defeat, but instead she would run, as hard as it may be, the not-so-beaten path of victory. And I had been given the divine opportunity to watch her run and to glean all that I could from this strong woman of God.

That is what I mean by not looking for friendship but instead simply living this life, one day at a time, allowing God to bring into my life, yes your life, those women whom he wants you to bless and be blessed by. Being content with having God as your friend is enough to show him that you need no one but him, and because of that contentment, he will bring good and life-long friends to you at just the right time.

The Measuring Stick

A sister in Christ once told me, "I knew I could trust you because you are not jealous of me." Wow! What a compliment. We as women spend so much time being jealous of other women that we can't become who God created us to be. We are jealous of everything from the way we look to the way we interact with our husbands, children, and other people. We're jealous of the way we keep house, the things we have, and the successes in our career or ministry. We're even jealous of our sisters' walk with the Lord. Rather than complimenting her on her dress or congratulating her on one of her successes, we look her up and down, roll our eyes at her, and then turn our head the other way, ignoring her. There is no way we're going to build her up or encourage her. You know what I'm talking about. It's time for a change because you are Woman Beautiful!

If you see yourself as unequal because of physical appearance, financial status, occupation, or any other difference, then you will never become who God created you to be. You are not measuring yourself by God's standard but by man's, or should I say woman's, standard. If you set yourself up as superior because of your physical appearance, financial status, occupation, or any other difference, then again you are not using God's measuring rod but your own: setting yourself up for failure, disappointment, and rejection. And if you're measuring other women by your own personal standard and not God's standard, then you will never help them become all that God created them to be either.

When a person judges another, there is one of two things going on: she has little to no esteem and carries hurt coupled with fear, or, she honestly believes, for whatever strange reason, that she is better or more right than the other person. More often than not, it is the former issue rather than the latter one. Yet in both circumstances, the woman does not understand her identity in Christ. The NIV translation of 2 Corinthians 10:12 puts a new light on the subject of exalting oneself: "We do not dare to classify or compare ourselves with some who commend themselves. When they measure themselves by themselves and compare themselves with themselves, they are not wise." Wow! That is role model revelation in a nutshell. Did you get that, Woman Beautiful? The woman which considers herself "superior" is deemed by God as being unwise. Don't be offended by her, don't be intimidated by her, and don't imitate her!

Christ is to be the only measuring stick—no one else. When we compare ourselves to him, we see just how

inadequate we really are. It is our duty as women of God to search out our own identities in Christ Jesus so that we can encourage other women in their personal womanhood. If we are busy being jealous, exalting ourselves or passing judgment, then we will never reach any level above mediocrity. We do not serve a mediocre God; we should not settle for mediocrity. Furthermore, we will never help the women in our spheres of influence rise above the status quo either.

Woman Beautiful, you are a child of the King, Almighty God. The book of Ephesians 4:12–13, NIV, says, "*We are to be prepared* as God's people for works of service, so that the body of Christ may be built up until we all reach unity in the faith and in the knowledge of the Son of God and become mature, attaining to the whole measure of fullness of Christ;" (my emphasis added). If you are still insecure in your identity, then you are immature in Christ Jesus. Our relationship with Jesus is a maturing process; therefore, it is imperative that we mature in Christ in order that we can live the abundant life he has ordained for us and so that we will bring glory to him.

We have no choice but to put down our own measuring sticks and hold a person up to Christ. When we do that, then we can see her with Christ's eyes and heart. We can ask ourselves, *Have I walked in her shoes?* If we've walked in her shoes, or better translated, "lived her life," then we can understand why she ticks the way she does. But when we ask that question, the answer will always be no and we, therefore, are incapable of fully understanding her many little quirks. We can only strive to love her as Christ loves her and determine in our own hearts to be the Christian sister God has called us to be. Not being jealous of her success, appearance, relationships, or anything else—just loving her in a God-glorifying way that will please him and build her up. We have been commissioned by God to make disciples of all (wo)men. Maturity on our part is letting the jealousy go so that we can help other women mature in Christ. You truly are Woman Beautiful!

Forgiveness

When is the last time you knowingly forgave a sister? Notice I didn't use the word "friend." It is easy to forgive a friend (if it's not easy, then she really wasn't your friend to begin with), but it's not so easy to forgive a sister in Christ who has offended you.

Your sin and my sin was such a heart-wrenching grievance for God that he had no choice but to make a way of forgiveness for us. The way he made was through his Son, Jesus Christ. God is purely perfect. There is no sin or refuse in him. Yet, he created a people that he wanted to and fully intended on spending eternity with. Being the divine and loving Creator that he is, it was in no way his desire to create a people that could not make their own choices, bearing the keen resemblance of robots, but a people that could either, by their will, choose him and his righteousness or reject him.

Forgiveness is a deliberate and obedient act of the will. God deliberately and willfully forgives each one of us as we come to him acknowledging Christ as his Son, seeking

that forgiveness, and inviting him into our lives to be our Lord and Savior. His genuine kindness toward us is the fruit of his forgiveness. You might ask, "What kindness?" That of deliverance from the penalty of an eternity spent in hell, the complete separation from him and others, the sweet, sweet kindness that is revealed so beautifully in the form of *daily* grace: the kindness that he shows us every day as we live out this life on earth.

Many people have explained grace as being "God's Riches at Christ's Expense." Let me take you a little bit deeper in the understanding of grace. To be given grace is to be given a full pardon. It is receiving what you really don't deserve. Our self-centered and sinful life really deserves the penalty of hell that God created for the devil and his demons. But, if man chooses to remain in sin and disobedience toward God, then he too will spend eternity in the state of complete separation from God and those people who have believed in Jesus. The word of God describes hell as being a bottomless pit, which would mean a constant feeling of falling; darkness, we all know that in the dark is where evil thrives; a lake of fire, which would be a constant sensation of intense physical pain; a place of isolation, so forget about partying in hell with your friends. You'll be falling in a dark, bottomless pit, isolated from those you love and who love you while in such excruciating pain that you will gnash your teeth with great grievance.

It is imperative that we be willing to forgive our sisters (and others who have hurt us) just as Christ has forgiven us. Forgiveness brings healing and restoration that is needed for wholeness. If Woman Beautiful does not forgive, she willingly sets herself up for problems, friendlessness, and emotional turmoil.

If you are the woman who struggles with forgiving others, then ask God to forgive your unwillingness to let go of the pain inflicted by others. Forgive the person(s), and act kindly toward this person in some way—and do it today! You will be opening yourself up to possible rudeness and insensitivity. Don't take it personally; you are a child of the King. Let him deal with that person.

Spending Time Together as Sisters in Christ

Moses enjoyed hanging out with God; spending time with him, learning more about him, and listening to his voice of love, patience, and instruction. God had called Moses to be the vessel that he would use to deliver his people from captivity in Egypt. Moses did indeed bring them out of Egypt, but he would not take them into the Promised Land. So after many years, Moses began a transition from leading the Israelite people to letting go of them. That transition would bring forth two men whom God considered to have followed him fully. (See Numbers 32:12.)

The man whom I am particularly intrigued with is Joshua. This man was as a sponge absorbing all of Yahweh that he could. On one occasion, while Moses was in the presence of God, speaking face-to-face with him, it came time to return to camp. But the young Joshua would not depart from the tent. (See Exodus 33:11.) It's interesting to me that Joshua would not depart from the tent even

after Moses had left. Perhaps he knew that in order to know God better it meant spending as much time with him as possible. I believe Joshua wanted to be where he knew God was.

Do you make it a priority to spend time with other women? Not just the women with whom you can relate to, but also those women whom you can minister to. Women want to be loved, accepted, befriended, and encouraged by other women, so Woman Beautiful has an amazing opportunity to let Christ shine through her by deliberately spending time with women who don't seem to fit the mold of the status quo. Just recently, my daughter Johnette said, "Mom, you have some weird friends." Well, my usual response would have been, "Cutie girl, we're all a little bit weird," but that day I responded differently: "It's because normal people don't like me." I thought our male friend sitting at our table was going to bust a gut with laughter. To quote Patsy Clairmont, "Normal *is* just a setting on a dryer." We're all a little bit different and a little bit weird, and to love and encourage those who seem to be just a little less than normal has to enlarge the heart of holy God. I've learned too much from my friends, who are tagged by many as being weird, to discount anything about them. Woman Beautiful, do not be afraid or ashamed to enjoy the company of those women who live life to their own sweet melody and to the beat of a totally different drum. God will bless you richly because of it!

My youngest daughter, Kendra, who was only fourteen at the time of this writing, puts it this way: "We're all a little weird; different. But if your different is different than my different, then that makes you the weird one." Rightly put, don't you agree? Woman Beautiful, God looks at each of us with all of our differences, quirks, and weird tendencies and willfully loves and accepts us. Shouldn't we do the same? Woman Beautiful, if you want to be befriended, then become one who intentionally befriends others, even those who are not-so-lovely.

> If you will cry with those who cry and rejoice with those who rejoice, then I (the Lord) will make sure that when it's your time to cry there will be those there to cry with you and when it is your time to rejoice there will be those there to rejoice with you.
>
> Marlene Mains, a word from the Lord.

Father, thank you for being my most valued friend. Thank you for giving me good friends at just the right times in my life: women whom I can confide in, be encouraged by, and delight in, and women whom I can trust. More than this, Lord, thank you for growing me into the Woman Beautiful you created me to be, loving those women who are different, accepting those women who fear being rejected, and encouraging those women who have not yet determined their full identity in Jesus Christ. Lord, today I set aside my own selfish wants and needs that I can love women without jealousy and without any expectations or fear. Lord, make me a vessel in which you use to glorify yourself and to build up those women around me. Father God, I need other women and they need me. Make me a powerful and effective tool that others will experience your love through me. Allow me to befriend every woman you put in my path.

Abba, Father, be glorified in me. In Jesus' more than able name, I pray. Amen.

Relating to Men (Who are Not Her Husband)

> "Her husband is known in the gates" (Proverbs 31:23, NAS).

Relating to men, other than your husband, is sometimes quite challenging. Women find it difficult at times to be kind and friendly without it being interpreted as flirting or inappropriate interest. It is very possible to have male friends but there are boundaries of protection that must be honored.

Setting Boundaries

Randy is a good friend of mine and that of my whole family. There are unspoken boundaries that we have set. Randy and I are both careful not to cross those boundaries: we do not touch, other than a friendly handshake when we've not seen one another for a long time; we pray for each other's spouse and family by name, and we encourage one another in the Lord. Almost every conversation that Randy and I have pertains either to our families, God, or money. (He is a financial advisor to John and me; that is how our friendship began.) If Randy or I were to choose to ignore the invisible boundaries set in our friend-friend relationship it would be a short road to an ended friendship.

The Bible has many examples of women who maintain healthy relationships with men other than their husbands. Lydia, for example, in Acts 16 was noted as hearing the Lord; therefore, opening her heart to the gospel and following him (Jesus Christ) in believer's baptism. Shortly after responding to the gospel, she "prevailed" upon Paul and Silas, persuading them to stay at her house. Her motives were pure, and I believe God gave Paul and Silas discernment to see the holy intentions of this new convert's heart. Through Lydia, the first organized church body of believers was established, and they held "church" gatherings in her home.

Rahab was an unlikely candidate for God to use in revealing his glory and fulfilling his purpose; nonetheless, he brought her into relationship with two strangers who were spying out the city of Jericho in order to take it. Being a harlot, she could have easily perversely "prevailed" upon the strangers, which would have corrupted God's intent. But out of set boundaries of both Rahab and the two spies, God blessed an entire nation. You can read her captivating story in Joshua 2:1–24 and Joshua 6:22–27.

All the men in town knew Rahab was good for one thing. Yet, notice how one woman, obedient unto God, can affect the kingdom of God when she acts with pure motives. Perhaps for the first time, she was providing for herself with an appropriate attitude and behavior and not with her body. Can you see it? The wall of Jericho lay in ruins except for one piece which housed the local prostitute, her precious mother and father, her brothers, and all of her father's household. God does amazing things

when men and women befriend each other with honored boundaries.

Let's look at Esther, a queen chosen because her predecessor refused to come to the king when summoned. Esther set her boundaries, listened closely to the instruction of those who had authority over her, and won the favor of *all* who "saw" her, especially the king. She then agreed to go before the king uninvited—which was sure death—on behalf of her people, but only if they would fast and pray for her and the reason for which she would petition the king. In wisdom and Godly strength, she prepared a banquet, invited the king, and revealed the plan of annihilation for the Jewish people. Amazingly, God honored Esther by placing the king on her side. Because Esther humbly honored those boundaries under the influence of the Lord, the Jewish people were spared. Esther knew her boundaries with the king, but more than that she knew the power of her God and the boundaries of prayer and fasting. *You too have been called to mature in beauty for such a time as this.* (See Esther 4:14.)

In each of these instances, *Christ* was the boundary line. When we set our boundary at him, maintaining our focus and remembering our commitment to Jesus, it becomes easier to relate to the men around us.

Words that Flatter

Proverbs 2:6–18 talks about the words women use toward men. It describes the woman who deliberately flatters men with her words as a strange and adulteress woman, a woman who leaves the companion of her youth and forgets the covenant of her God.

There is a time and place for flattering and flirting: before you're married and to an unmarried and unattached man. It is also important that you continue flattering and flirting with your husband until death do you part.

It doesn't matter if you and your husband said your vows in front of a Justice of the Peace, in a church, or in an Elvis-styled chapel in Las Vegas, God ordained marriage, therefore, you made your wedding vow not only to your husband but also to him.

Difficulty in marriage, unfulfilled expectations, unmet needs, and self-centered attitudes move many women to look to other men. Hoping to have these needs met, she forgets the marriage covenant she made not only to her husband before many witnesses but, more importantly to God.

The Bible calls a woman who flatters with her tongue and flirts with her eyes an adulterous woman. An adulterous woman paves the way of her own destruction and that of her family. In fact, the word says she causes her house to sink down to death and her tracks lead to death. A woman who flirts with a man other than her husband leads her own household into death and destruction. A marriage can take many turns that lead to destruction but, show me a marriage or household falling apart, and I will almost always show you a wife or husband inappropriately interacting with the opposite sex.

Many women are looking for love, fulfilling sex, and understanding in the wrong places and ways. Are you this

woman? Ask God to reveal your real needs to you and teach you how to convey those needs to your husband. He will be faithful to lead you in that communication, but if your husband refuses to hear you and make necessary changes do not despair, God will show you his faithfulness. You'll learn and begin to believe that all of your needs *can* be met by God. I've found in my own marriage that my expectations in John might never be met nor, should they be. God's expectations for him, on the other hand, can and will be met if I will commit to pray for him and wait for those changes in kindness and love expressed toward him. God's expectation for your husband will be realized also if you will pray that God would graciously mature him into the man he created him to be.

If you'll pray fervently for yourself, while you're in the waiting, he will work amazing changes in you. Trust the Lord to meet your needs, pray earnestly for yourself, and you will become the woman of God that he created you to be. He will not disappoint you.

Rest assured, "The heartfelt prayer of a righteous (wo)man is powerful and effective" (James 5:16) (my paraphrase).

Proper Dress

Because we know that men are visual, it is important that we are modest in the way we dress. It surprises me at what causes men to think lustful thoughts about women—much of which is innocent behavior on our part. For example, it is suggested that women not carry their purse or bag around their neck in such a way that the strap crosses between their breasts. I would have never considered this a problem for men, except I heard a man talking about it (as he was a recovering porn addict, *a man once caught up in sexual sin*) on our local Christian radio station. I even thought, *Whatever!* But on one occasion my husband made a comment on how my seat belt split my boobs, I knew then that it was for real. Yes, men have the problem, but we need to be conscious of those around us as not to fuel their sin problems.

Before you interject the well-known lie, "God made men that way," let me correct that with what is really true. God created Adam to look at his wife and be wowed, even intrigued by her beauty. There was no sin or perversion in it. At the fall, man began to lust, and it was at that time that he began his struggle with the sinful desire for women. If men want to believe the long-told and accepted lie that *God made them* in such a way that they would look at women other than their wives and get excited then so be it, but Woman Beautiful, it is time that you choose not to believe it or be controlled by it. Men are visually aroused sexually, but that visual arousal can and should be controlled in and through the power of the Holy Spirit.

How self-rationalizing and ridiculous is it that we would accuse God of making such a flaw in man. But until men learn to take that aspect of the fall captive, we women have to do our part in not feeding their temptation. Do you hear what I'm saying, Woman Beautiful? Don't fall for the lie any longer, but don't feed the sin problem either.

Woman Beautiful needs to evaluate why she dresses

the way she does. Is there an underlying issue that needs to be dealt with? Most women dress for women, not men. We want to look as good or better than the women we're going to be around. Not because of what it's going to do to man, but because we subconsciously think, *How are the women around me going to perceive and receive me?* Could it be that Woman Beautiful's self-esteem has been wounded because of something in childhood or marriage? Perhaps she was never told she was pretty. Or quite possibly her sisters were always getting the compliments. Maybe she was overweight and perhaps still is. Could it be that many of us were sexually abused or maybe Daddy wasn't interactive in our lives? It could even be that our husbands take long, regular looks at women who are shapelier than we are. A thousand different reasons as to why women dress the way they do exist, but we need to dress for God, our husbands, and ourselves.

God does not want you to be a stumbling block, nor does he want you to be the object of any other man's obsession. Even though your husband may like your clothes a little tight or short, save that dress for your private times. He will love it! And you, Woman Beautiful, need to feel good, especially on the inside. Feeling good on the inside always means showing less on the outside. Let me do say this: I have a friend who once said, "I've finally decided that my boobs are going to stick out. There is nothing I can do about it." She is so right! Buy clothes that fit right and that you feel good in. Use good judgment. If you're not sure, ask the Holy Spirit; he will let you know what appropriate attire is, and what it is not.

The Apostle Paul talks to women about their dress, and his warning to us was not to prevent us from looking our best; instead, it was to encourage us to dress appropriately on all occasions—especially in the presence of other men—as not to be a stumbling block to them or a shame to our husbands. (See 1 Timothy 2:9.) And in Peter's writings, he instructed us to dress not for show, but to put on the imperishable quality of a gentle and quiet spirit, which is precious in the sight of God. (See 1 Peter 3:3–4.) Both Paul and Peter turn our attention to what is truly attractive: the eternal beauty of the inner woman.

Don't get entangled in legalism here. Modest dress includes not showing too much skin: cleavage, leg, midriff, or lower back. Be careful when it comes to uncovered shoulders as well. It also means to use good judgment in the tightness of fit.

Woman Beautiful, take a look through your closet. Are there pieces of clothing hanging there that need to be trashed? Not sold or given away, but trashed as not to make other women stumbling blocks either. Determine the reasons why you dress the way you do, then make the necessary changes to your wardrobe in order to dress as the Woman Beautiful God created you to be.

Lord, I stand in awe of your greatness and of who you are. You amaze me. Father, when I am tempted to seek those needs a woman has outside of my relationship with you or with my husband, stop me! Remind me of your unfailing love and of the covenant that you established with me, that covenant of being my God, my ever present help in time of trouble or need—the covenant that you made saying, "She will be my

people and I will be her God," when I accepted Christ as my personal Lord and Savior. Father, lead me in the path of your righteousness that I will not walk the path of death, nor will I take my family down it. Holy God, teach me how to interact with those men who are not my husband. Enable me always to set the boundary at Jesus that your will would be done and that you would be glorified. In Jesus' name, I pray. Amen.

Beauty Tips

1. Ask God for a woman prayer partner whom you can bare your heart to.
2. Ask your husband how you can show him respect.
3. Memorize Isaiah 54:5
4. Ask God to forgive you for not responding to both your husband and others with a gentle and quiet spirit.
5. Confess your sin of disrespect toward your husband and repent so God will enable you to submit in respect to your husband and obedience to God.
6. Pray specifically for each of your children or those in your sphere of influence by name and for the plan God has for them.
7. Pray for each of your children by name asking God to reveal their gifts and talents to you and to them.
8. Call those things that are not as though they already were.
9. Speak God's truth to, about, and over your children.

10. Remind yourself regularly that things are not as they appear and that the devil is a liar.
11. Intentionally contact a woman whom you've not been able to get acquainted with or whom God reveals to you as needing a friend. Simply send her a "God brought you to mind card," call her by phone, see her in person, or send her an email.
12. Act kindly toward all women.
13. Make a prayer log of five women you can pray for daily. Choose women who've offended you, seem to be snobbish, are quiet or withdrawn, and most importantly, who do not know the Lord. Be faithful to pray for them daily.
14. Remember, you've not walked in any woman's shoes but your own.
15. Willfully forgive one woman who has offended you.
16. Consider how you relate to the men in your life: does your behavior glorify the Lord?
17. Make necessary changes: quit talking to certain men if you need to, set your boundary at Christ, determine to display a life of godly purity.
18. Ask God to meet your emotional, affectionate, and physical needs.
19. Make necessary changes in your dress: not too tight, not too short, and not too revealing.
20. Ask God to never let you be the object of another man's obsession.

Spiritual Beauty

"But a woman who fears the LORD, she shall be praised" (Proverbs 31:30, NAS).

Step Three

Be Intimate with God

If Woman Beautiful wants to walk into the most fruitful, beautifully decorated life, she first has to step into a relationship with God. This step of beauty is the most important and powerful step you will take. It is also the easiest. God will make you Woman Beautiful, changing you from the inside out!

God created us because he wanted someone in his likeness that he could have fellowship with, someone he could be intimate with and enjoy as well as someone who would enjoy him. God wanted a relationship with us, yet God is holy; and because he is holy, he hates sin; he hates it so much that when we sin, it separates us from him. With that in mind, we can understand how important it is to stay in right relationship with God. We know the absolute necessity in striving for a sinless life and lifestyle in order that we would be "holy because he is holy." (See Leviticus 11:44, Ephesians 4:1, and 1 Peter 1:16.)

Spiritual beauty is summed up in Woman Beautiful's personal walk with God, taking him at his word and obeying him. God did not create you a robot being programmed with limited and controlled behavior, but he gave you a mind, body, and spirit, therefore giving you the privilege to choose. It is only by your choice that God enjoys sweet fellowship with you and you with him. Make the choice today to know him better and love him more by deliberately spending time with him. You are Woman Beautiful!

Knowing Jesus

If you know Jesus Christ as your personal Lord and Savior, then God's word to you is this: "You are now a new creation, you are a new person; the old ways you used to live and think and walk and talk and do are now gone. There is a whole new you ready to emerge." Hallelujah! (My paraphrase of 2 Corinthians 5:17.)

Perhaps you have been a Christian for most of your life. Has the new you been able to emerge? Or are you just being content with the way you are, accepting your personality as simply being the way God created you? Too many times, Woman Beautiful gets into the habit of doing the church thing she's always done, and it doesn't even occur to her that God has more and better things for her—that he might want to raise her up a notch or two, raising her standards of loving a little bit higher. Perhaps convicting her of the destructive effects gossip, and other sins committed against his creation, has on the high calling of expressing love.

Many of us write off gossiping as no big deal. We call passing judgment—by our standard—holy righteousness. We call other sin such things as homosexuality, mental illness, alcoholism, drug addiction, abuse, busyness, depression, being an introvert, and anything else in order to keep from admitting that we might be caught up in sin. Don't get me wrong, these are very real issues, but Scripture calls them sin, demon oppression, and carnality. Whether you are a brand new Christian or have been one for thirty years, God still wants that new creature in you to be constantly emerging.

There is a lie that Satan has very cunningly told God's people. Many of you have received the lie and aren't even aware of it. The lie includes not having to go to church, read the Bible, or even pray in order to be a Christian. You might argue that this is true, but really it is only half true, and a half-truth equals a whole lie. A Christian is one who follows Christ, and not only that, but a Christian is one who strives for complete obedience toward God. I suppose if you wanted to just muddle through life temporarily stagnant then quickly declining in your spiritual walk, you could not go to church, not read your Bible, and not pray; but Christ said that he had come to give life to the fullest. If you desire the full life that God intends for you, then you must become a Christ-follower. You have to spend time with him, in his word, prayer, and worship as well as with other believers. Then, you have to put into practice that which he teaches you through his Holy Spirit, his word, and other born-again, Spirit-filled believers. There is a big difference between being "saved" and being a God-glorifying Christian living a life of abundance and joy. Which do you want to be?

Spiritual beauty is all about your relationship with God. It is being changed a little bit more every day. It is being more holy today then you were last year and being more holy next year than you are today. Sister, you cannot grow in the likeness and glory of God if you are not spending time with him. It cannot be done. Quit believing the lie!

The Triune God

God is one person with three entities. He is God the Father, God the Son, and God the Holy Spirit. It is vital that you know and understand each person of the Trinity, understanding his role in both eternity and time. He is one God, yet three persons. We were created in his three images: God being the mind, Christ being the body, and the Holy Spirit being the spirit. Because we have been created in the likeness of his three separate entities—mind, body, and spirit—we can know him intimately. We are capable of understanding him, relating to him, and knowing his desires for both our lives and his Kingdom. We can recognize his voice when he speaks to us; we can know his heart, therefore, we can know what he expects of his children.

God, the Mind

The first person of the Godhead is God himself. He calls himself by such names as Holy Father, King of glory, Lord God Almighty, Lord Most High, Lord, and Creator of heaven and earth. He describes his character as "faithful God who does no wrong," (Deuteronomy 32:4); "Father of the fatherless and Judge for the widows," (Psalm 68:5); "my Helper," (Psalm 118:7); "my Confidence," (Psalm 71:5); and "my Hiding Place" (Psalm 32:7). Even though the names and character traits listed are just a few, I believe you can understand that God is able to be, and longs to be, all things to all people.

God has more recently been acknowledged by many scientists as being the intelligent designer behind this intelligently designed universe. He is a God of order and purpose. There is an order in which everything takes place or is formed. He divinely created an orderly universe capable of expansion; a civilization that can think, feel, and reason; and he developed a relationship format that glorifies him and brings purpose to our being. Apart from superior, infallible, and infinite intelligence, this universe could not have come into existence and we could not have been so intricately designed.

The universe has been proven to be constantly expanding. It is safe to say that God is a god of more. He is completely limitless. 1 Timothy 2:5, Exodus 3:15, Isaiah 44:8, and Deuteronomy 4:39 identify God as the "self-existent one." He has always been, he will always be, and as the universe expands, so does his purpose for you.

His intellect surpasses all of mans. We are limited in our thinking, reasoning, and achievement only by the perception we hold of Holy God and the level of determined faith we are willing to exercise.

Woman Beautiful, what holds you back from becoming all God created you to be?

You are now a new creation. You are a new person. The old ways you used to live and think and walk and talk and do are now gone—even those behaviors and attitudes of yesterday. There is a whole new you ready to emerge. Hallelujah! God's desire for you is constant, continuous expansion—increase in every area of your life.

Rather than rationalizing sin as "just being the way a person is," in order to keep from admitting that we might be caught up in sin, it is time to really get to know God and understand just exactly how his intellect classifies our sin, the sin which a person covets is nothing more than putting her own desires before God's. Seeking after one's own self-serving way is a form of carnality, and to be carnal is to have a lust for the world. This lust depicts a behavior resembling that of a lower nature. Animalistic-lust for worldly prizes, possessions, and promotions, causes a person to slide deeper into a sin-filled lifestyle; therefore, becoming enslaved to her fleshly desires. Some people try to rationalize sinful behavior as being merely human but, by God's standard of holiness, any sin is ravenous, harmful and leads to death. Rationalized sinful behavior determines the difference between maturing in Christ and looking like the lost, dead world.

No matter where you are in Christ, it is time to step it up a notch. As I said earlier, spiritual beauty is all about your relationship with God. It is being changed a little bit more every day. It is being more holy today then you were last year and being more holy next year than you are today. Beloved Woman Beautiful, you cannot grow in the likeness and glory of God if you are not spending time with him or deliberately striving for a life of holiness. Because God is holy, it cannot be done. *Quit believing the lie!* The Bible says, in Romans 12:2, that we are to "no longer be

conformed to the likeness of the world but we are to be transformed by the renewing of our minds."

Dr. Charles Stanley says, "If you are not spending time in the Bible every day, then you are suffering from malnutrition." Any living thing that is not fed dies. To possess God's intellect—his knowledge, wisdom, and understanding—begins with feeding the living spirit within you. This regular feeding renews your mind, transforming you into the likeness of Christ.

Jesus, the Body

Just as Christ is the physical being of God, so have we been created in his physical likeness. Woman Beautiful, your body is God's dwelling place. The way you treat it is a direct reflection of the way you respect God.

Christ deliberately and willfully, knowingly gave his life for your and my ransom. His body was holy and set apart to be God's from the beginning of forever. It was through his physical body that God accomplished his purpose.

God's intentions for you include your physical body. It may be healthy, sickly, large, or small, but God cannot use you effectively if you refuse to accept your body as his temple, his beautiful building, his dwelling place. Taking care of the only body you have is vital to God's purpose for your life.

Christ's body was the sacrifice he would eventually make for you and me. Perfectly average, but set apart for God's solemn purpose; strong enough to withstand the brutal beating, yet frail enough to merit the gentle washing of his feet. His body was the dwelling place of Almighty God and the temple that would be broken down and raised again in three days.

Just as Christ surrendered his body to the purposes and plan of God, so should we. The word of God says that our bodies are his temple, his dwelling place. It should be our purpose and goal to maintain our bodies in such a way that they will be most useable by him.

Christ, the Perfect God/Man Sacrifice

The truth about Christ is that he was born to die. That is, to die for you and me. His body, which was perfectly average, was willfully given by both him and his Father in order that we could have eternal life in heaven with them. This provision includes coming into a relationship with him by surrendering our lives to Jesus.

There are those who will argue, "You cannot be saved without saying the sinner's prayer." To the best of my knowledge, there was no such recorded prayer in the first century church that had to be prayed. We were only instructed to "confess with our mouths that Jesus Christ is Lord and believe in our hearts that God raised Him from the dead and we would be saved" (Romans 10:9). The sinners' prayer is a way of confessing to God one's belief in the truth of Romans 10:9, therefore, receiving Jesus Christ as Lord. Woman Beautiful has to believe this life-changing truth in her heart before she *can* confess Jesus as Lord with her mouth. She has to believe in her heart that Jesus is the

Son of God whom he raised from the dead. For many, the heart change has all ready occurred before the prayer has ever been prayed; yet, the prayer to receive Christ as your personal Savior and Lord is powerful and life changing. I highly recommend that you pray a prayer confessing this to God.

If you've never placed your faith in him, asking Jesus to be your Lord and Savior, today is the day to do it! There is nothing that you have ever done or that has been done to you that keeps him from loving you, forgiving you, and saving you. Go to the end of this chapter and say the prayer confessing your sins to Jesus, asking him to become your Lord and Savior. Express your desire to be filled with his Holy Spirit. Tell him that you wholly surrender and commit to him.

Holy Spirit, the Spirit

The Holy Spirit is God "still" on earth. He has been given to us that we could commune with God, know him, and be empowered to live a life of victory that brings glory to him. He is all around us and wants to dwell in us.

At salvation, we are sealed with the Holy Spirit and cannot for any reason lose our salvation. (See Ephesians 1:13.) But we are not necessarily filled with the Holy Spirit. In a water baptism, a person is totally submerged. The same is true for the baptism of the Holy Spirit. When we are baptized in the Holy Spirit, we are totally submerged in him. It is in this submerging that we are empowered for the great and awesome works of almighty God.

Although I believe scripture teaches that the baptism of the Holy Spirit comes after water baptism, I am convinced for some that baptism comes immediately at the time of believing; for others it can be years down the road, and yet for others it may never be.

It is by the Spirit that we insist on God's way, not our own. It is by the Holy Spirit that we detest sin. It is by the Holy Spirit that we eagerly share the gospel of Christ. It is by the Holy Spirit that we dare to dream dreams bigger than ourselves. And it is by the Spirit that we are able to love God with all our heart, mind, soul, and strength. It is also by the Spirit that we are able to love our neighbor no matter what race, gender, economic status, age, or religion they may be, as ourselves.

The Holy Spirit in a person cannot allow that person to stay the way she was when she first came into relationship with Christ; his purpose is to reveal more of God to the individual in order that she would become more like him. If you are not motivated to change and become like Christ, then one of two things has happened: you have either never really trusted in Christ as your personal Savior and Lord and you're just believing a lie you've told yourself, or you've never given the gentleman first place in your life: embracing the lordship of God by yielding to the Holy Spirit and his power for your life.

The word of God says, "Narrow is the gate *of righteousness and holiness,* and few take it. But broad is the gate of *godlessness and many take it*" (Matthew 7:13–14, NAS) (my emphasis added). Perhaps you are really walking the broad road of godlessness. Perhaps you prayed the

sinner's prayer once and thought that was the end of your conversion. It was not! God intends fully for you to become more like Christ in the way you love and live, think and reason. One of my favorite quotes is from the late but well-known Dr. Bill Bright, founder of Campus Crusade for Christ: "We should live our lives in such a way that when we cross over into heaven God has very little changing to do." This is probably one of the most profound statements I have ever heard. What Dr. Bright was saying is that we should be so intentional in getting to know God by way of the Holy Spirit and the written word that we live our lives in such a way we look so much like Christ that God has almost no changing to do in us, in the perfecting process, when we cross over into heaven.

If you are trying to live your life by relying on your own understanding and intellect, then you could very easily be doing nothing more than living similarly to the world while claiming to be Christian. Evaluate what kind of Christian woman you are and what kind you want to be: one excited about living for the awesome and holy True God, walking a life of victory and fullness as you mature in Jesus, or one still being the victim, wondering why God allows people to be so hurtful, stupid, and mean. Determine to spend time with him daily and to participate regularly in the fellowship of other believers; watch God change you and your life from the inside out.

Know the Holy Spirit and His Role in the Trinity

It is to our advantage that Christ ascended into heaven because the Holy Spirit would not have been sent. (See John 16:7.) The word teaches us that Jesus calls the Holy Spirit our helper who was sent by God. God sent him in the name of Jesus, and his mission is to teach you all things about God and godly living and to bring to your remembrance everything that Christ teaches you in Scripture. (See John 14:26.)

It was not until after his water baptism and his Holy Spirit baptism that Jesus did any recorded miracles. The Holy Spirit empowered him from that day forward to heal the sick, prophesy, deliver the afflicted from demonic possession, give sight to the blind, raise the dead, and other amazing miracles.

We can see when Jesus received the Holy Spirit, and it was not when he confessed that God was his Father or Lord; he began doing that, as recorded in the written word, at age twelve. It was after he had been baptized. If you're not familiar with his baptism, read Matthew 3:13–17 to get a beautiful picture of the account.

> Then Jesus arrived from Galilee at the Jordan coming to John, to be baptized by him.
>
> But John tried to prevent him, saying, "I have need to be baptized by you, *and yet,* you come to me?" But Jesus answering said to him, "*Baptize me* at this time; for in this way it is fitting for us to fulfill all righteousness." *Then John baptized him.* After

> being baptized, Jesus came up immediately from the water; and behold, the heavens were opened, and he saw the Spirit of God descending as a dove and lighting on him, and behold, a voice out of the heavens said, "This is my beloved Son, in whom I am well-pleased" (My paraphrase added).

I am convinced that Christ received the Holy Spirit at the time in his life when he could finally say: *I am totally about you, Father, nothing but you.* Many will argue that Christ was always about God, and I agree with that, but Christ was the first-born son. A Jewish-born son carried a load of responsibilities. I believe the first thirty years of his life were years of preparation for his ministry; those years included honoring his earthly father and mother, studying the then written word of God, praying and meditating on the Lord. He can relate to us so well because he lived life as we do with all the frustrations, temptations, and demands. It was not until he could leave his earthly father's home that he would pour his whole being into the purpose that God intended for him.

As comfortable as it is to say that we get all we're going to get when we invite Jesus into our hearts, Scripture shows us that the mighty empowerment of the Holy Spirit can come before we ask Christ to be our Savior as well as immediately upon asking him, or even days, weeks, months, and for some years after inviting him in.

Let's look at a few passages of scripture that bring light to this person, the Holy Spirit:

While Peter was still speaking these words, the Holy Spirit fell upon all those who were listening to the message. All the circumcised believers who came with Peter were amazed, because the gift of the Holy Spirit had been poured out on the Gentiles also. For they were hearing them speaking with tongues and exalting God. Then Peter answered, "Surely no one can refuse the water for these to be baptized who have received the Holy Spirit just as we did, can he?" And he ordered them to be baptized in the name of Jesus Christ. Then they asked him to stay for a few days.

Acts 10:44–48 (NAS)

Now when the apostles in Jerusalem heard that Samaria had received the word of God, they sent them Peter and John, who came down and prayed for them that they might receive the Holy Spirit. For He had not yet fallen upon any of them; they had simply been baptized in the name of the Lord Jesus. Then they began laying their hands on them, and they were receiving the Holy Spirit.

Acts 8:14–17 (NAS)

It happened that while Apollos was at Corinth, Paul passed through the upper country and came to Ephesus, and found some disciples. He said to them, "Did you receive the Holy Spirit when you believed?" And they said to him, "No, we have not even heard whether there is a Holy Spirit." And

> he said, "Into what then were you baptized?" And they said, "Into John's baptism."
>
> Paul said, "John baptized with the baptism of repentance, telling the people to believe in Him who was coming after him, that is in Jesus." When they heard this they were baptized in the name of the LORD Jesus. And when Paul had laid his hands upon them, the Holy Spirit came on them, and they began speaking with tongues and prophesying.
>
> Acts 19:1–6 (NAS)

It would be self-exalting and ridiculous for any one of us to limit God on how he can or cannot impart the Holy Spirit on believers. What is important for us to know here is that God *is* sovereign and he can do whatever he wants, whenever he wants, however he wants. He is God all by himself, and if he chooses to impart the Holy Spirit on one person as she prays the prayer of salvation and on another person after she's been a Christian for many years and yet another person before she ever utters the sinner's prayer, then so be it. What is important is that at some time in our lives we get to the point where we want our lives to be all about God and not about ourselves. The person with this mindset and heart condition is the person whom God liberally pours his Spirit on.

I heard a Baptist preacher once say, "I don't understand the filling of the Holy Spirit the way my charismatic friends do, but I believe it." For many mainstream denominations, the Holy Spirit is someone who is more thought about than taught about; because so many people are afraid of the Baptism of the Holy Spirit, or perhaps they believe the long-told half-truth of, "You get all of God that you are going to get when you accept Christ as your Lord and Savior." But more than likely many refuse to receive the Holy Spirit's baptism because they simply have never experienced it or because they didn't know there was such a thing. Or perhaps they believe the other half-truth that claims, *a person who has the baptism of the Holy Spirit has to speak in tongues,* and they do not, therefore, they must not have the Holy Spirit, or worse there must not be any such thing as the baptism of the Holy Spirit.

Let me help you sort through the confusion that has been needlessly caused by too many right-winged, left-winged, and no-winged believers.

There have been those groups who have insisted that you can be saved without having the indwelling filling of the Holy Spirit. That, I believe, as we have seen in the above referenced scripture is true, but not because he is uninvited or unwanted, but because the believer is ignorant about him. Those same groups of believers claim that you cannot have the indwelling of the Holy Spirit without speaking in tongues. That, I believe, is scripturally incorrect. There are many passages that speak of the Holy Spirit and his filling, not only mentioning tongues but also the other spiritual gifts that are imparted into believers by the Holy Spirit. Only to some does he give the gifts of tongues, just as only some receive the gift of prophecy, miracles, knowledge, and the many other spiritual gifts.

There is another group of believers that claim tongues, prophecy, miracles, and like gifts were only distributed in

the days of Jesus and shortly thereafter his death. In my opinion, this group of believers will stand in judgment before Holy God for taking away from the truth of his written word. There is nowhere in Scripture that says spiritual gifts were for the days of old. In fact, it says the opposite: "'And it shall be in the last days,' God says, 'that I will pour forth of my spirit on all mankind *(all races of men);* and your sons and your daughters shall prophesy, and your young men shall see visions, and your old men shall dream dreams; even on my bondslaves, both men and women, I will in those days pour forth of my spirit And they shall prophesy'" (Acts 2:17–18, NAS) (my emphasis added). Whenever I hear a Bible teacher say, "Prophecy is a thing of the past," I want to holler, *Ugh! Don't you know the word of God!* Or when I hear another declare, "You can't have the baptism of the Holy Spirit without speaking in tongues," I want to stand up and say, *What Bible do you read?* And when I hear a preacher who's struggling with believing *all* of God's word say, "You get all of the Holy Spirit that you're going to get when you invite Jesus into your heart," I want to gently say, *Won't you dare to go deeper?* We do indeed receive all of him at salvation but we do not receive a *full measure* of him at that same time.

God is indeed a God of more. If he imparted all of himself on a person at salvation, that person would be so overwhelmed she would either die or run. As we grow in our walk, God "releases," if you will, a little more of himself on those of us who want more.

What I have concluded is that many, many believers have placed too much trust in what their Bible teachers have believed and taught, therefore, placing little value in the teachings of Rabboni, Jesus Christ, the true teacher.

The apostle Paul was totally submerged in the Holy Spirit upon believing in Christ as Messiah. Under the influence of the Spirit, he writes in 1 Corinthians 12:7–11, an excellent description of what gifts the Holy Spirit imparts on believers and how he imparts them:

> But to each one is given the manifestation of the Spirit for the common good. For to one is given the word of wisdom through the Spirit, and to another the word of knowledge according to the same Spirit; to another faith by the same Spirit, and to another gifts of healing by the one Spirit, And to another the effecting of miracles, and to another prophecy, and to another the distinguishing of spirits, to another various kinds of tongues, and to another the interpretation of tongues. But one in the same Spirit works all these things, distributing to each one individually just as He wills.

The different gifts of the Holy Spirit are manifested in each of us differently for the common good of God's people, and they are given to us as *he* wills. For too many years, mainstream denominations have ignored the gifts or claimed they were for the days of the Bible times rather than accepting them as gifts from God to be used today in promoting the common good of his people. More and more, we are hearing charismatic preachers and teachers say that "the gift of tongues is *an* evidence of the indwelling Holy Spirit," not "*the*" evidence, and I am shouting *praise*

God! It is time that we as believers quit trying to limit God on what he can and can't impart on his own people and start working toward building up the body of Christ. *All* spiritual gifts have been and are given by the same Spirit for the *common good of the body of Christ!* Remember, they are manifested in individual believers according to God's will and plan.

In light of the scriptures we have read in this chapter, could it still be possible today that many of us are baptized in the name of the Lord with water only and not with the Holy Spirit? The Holy Spirit has been given to us so that we could commune with God. He is all around us, on us, and wants to dwell in us. Your heart-felt burning desire to obey God, know him better, and love him more will open the door for a Holy Spirit filling like you have never experienced before.

Remember I said earlier, "It is by the Spirit that one insists on God's way, not her own. It is by the Holy Spirit that she detests sin, especially her own. It is by the Holy Spirit that Woman Beautiful eagerly shares the gospel of Christ. It is by the Holy Spirit that she dares to dream dreams bigger than herself, and it is by the Spirit that she is able to love God with all of her heart, mind, soul, and strength, and her neighbor as herself." She no longer looks at a sister and makes the deliberate choice to "not like her" but rather the Spirit-filled Woman Beautiful looks at her sister and says, "Lord, let me see her with your eyes that I will love her well."

Do you get what I am saying? If you possess little to none of the character of Christ or his purpose for your life stated in the previous paragraph, perhaps you need to release God to work in you in a whole new way. Perhaps you need to ask him to submerge you in his Spirit that you would walk securely in the power, conviction, and joy of Holy God. If you are still the same today in the way you relate to God and others as you were the day you asked Christ to be your Savior, then perhaps you need to ask him to baptize you with his Holy Spirit. Hopefully, by now you are tired of an unproductive Christian walk. Perhaps you are ready to live totally for *him!*

The word of God says that we, spirit-filled, born-again believers, will be known by our fruit and by our love. Is your love walk one that glorifies God? Does it esteem others? Or is it a walk that is consumed by self and self-glorification? How about the fruit that you bear? Is it the irresistible fruit of the Holy Spirit: love, joy, peace, patience, kindness, goodness, gentleness, faithfulness, and self-control? (See Galatians 5:22–23.)

What about the gifts of the Spirit? Is one or perhaps some of them growing in you? They are: prophecy, service, teaching, exhortation, giving, leadership, mercy, gifts of healing, knowledge, wisdom, various tongues, effects of miracles, discernment (or distinguishing of spirits), preaching, evangelizing, faith, and acts of worship. (See 1 Corinthians 12.)

There are two spiritual gifts that every born-again believer has been given without exception: the gift of worship and the gift of love. Both of these gifts, like the others, only manifest to the level at which we are willing to believe and trust God.

Isn't it interesting how we condemn others for raising

their hands, clapping, and even dancing during worship? Or how we look down on others who show loving kindness to the *not so lovely?* Have you ever considered that the reason why some people condemn other people as they practice their gifts is because those doing the condemning have not allowed their gifts to manifest in such a way that they can understand the freedom that other believers enjoy: the freedom to worship God and love others in sold out abandonment as the Holy Spirit leads.

Perhaps they have been conditioned to be expressionless before the Lord because of denomination-inflicted religion. If a person doesn't have the gift of tongues, they confidently say it was for the days of old; or if someone doesn't have the gift of prophecy, they say that prophecy stopped when Jesus was raised from the dead. The gift of discernment sometimes gets passed off as "gut feeling." To physically worship the Lord with the lifting of hands, clapping, and even dancing tags a person as a "holy roller" or a little weird at best, and to love unconditionally gets a person placed in lower class status. But the truth is that God is the same yesterday, today, and forever. He still manifests his gifts in his children to be used for the common good of the whole body as well as to glorify God.

If you indeed are a Spirit-filled believer, then you should be seeing yourself grow in the fruits and *gifts* of the Spirit. If not, perhaps you don't have quite the connection with God you think you have; you may want to prayerfully consider asking the Lord to baptize you with his Spirit, emptying you out and totally submerging you with and in his sweet, sweet Spirit.

Perhaps you are a new Christian and aren't yet seeing

many of these gifts; please don't think I've said you're not saved or that you're not filled with the Holy Spirit. If you have placed your faith in Jesus Christ, receiving him as your Savior, then you in fact are sealed for eternity. Yet, you may not be fully equipped. Remember what Bill Bright said: "We should live our lives in such a way that when we cross over into heaven God has very little changing to do." Living your life in this way demands total immersion in and by the Holy Spirit; you cannot live a life rich in the fruit and gifts of the Spirit apart from him.

My Personal Testimony

I accepted Christ as my personal Savior and Lord at the age of nine. I distinctly remember the very first step I took toward the altar. I believe it was then that Christ entered into my heart. Energized with peace and joy, I walked the aisle. Because I was young, my pastor wanted to make sure I knew what I was doing; he wanted to talk with me in his office at another time. A few days later, I went into his office and he began a conversation with me concerning the "Roman Road": a method of sharing the gospel of Christ. I remember being very excited since the first step I took toward Christ on the previous Sunday morning. I prayed the prayer of salvation, I think to satisfy my pastor, and went home.

I loved church and everything about it. I had already begun loving the Lord but was not yet aware that it was a relationship which God had initiated with me.

A couple of years passed and all seemed to be well

until our ball of fire, red-headed pastor left our church for another one. The difficulties of church *stuff* began to take place, and my family gradually slowed in our church attendance. So when we moved to Arkansas a year later, it made it easy to quit going to church altogether.

At about the age of thirteen, I knew I was "different" or, should I say, "called" by God for an unrevealed purpose, although I didn't recognize it as a call until many years later. As I entered my teen years, I began a life of rebellion, mostly against God, in the form of blatant worldly sin. You may know what I'm talking about: alcohol, drugs, and premarital sex. By the time I was nineteen, I knew there was something missing in my life but didn't know just what.

At age twenty, I had gone from being an unwed mother and was now married to the father of my little girl. He was an abusive alcoholic, and life with him had become absolute hell. After an argument that turned physical on New Year's Eve 1994, I moved back into my parent's home.

In early February of '95, my daughter and I were sitting on my parent's bed when I looked over and saw a pile of books lying on the floor. One of the books had a picture with two people backpacking on it. I could only read a portion of the title; it said, *Survival Kit.* Curiosity kicked in immediately; I couldn't imagine what my parents were doing with a book about backpacking. When I picked up the book, the rest of the title read, *For New Christians.* I opened the book and read the first paragraph and thought to myself, *this is what I've been looking for.* In that instant, the Holy Spirit fell on me. The room was filled with the presence of Holy God. I began to laugh and cry, and the peace of the Presence was unbelievable. I had no idea what had happened, but when I woke the next morning I knew my life had been changed by God for forever.

He initiated a divine encounter with me and changed me for eternity from the inside out. I have never looked back! He impacted me in such a way that when I began asking and seeking, God began doing, and my faith has only grown stronger. I knew I was different on the inside, and from that time on, I would be his for the rest of my earthly life as well as throughout eternity. What he did in me in that one brief moment changed me more than the day I received Christ as my Savior. I can't explain it, but I believe now that the amazing encounter was indeed the baptism of the Holy Spirit. On that night, he made two things clear to me: I am valuable to him and there is certainly more to being Christian than what I had. I am convinced that many Christians have no more than what I had: *salvation in Christ Jesus yet, an unexplainable desire and need of something more.*

I believe the fire of God fell on me that night, and there is nothing that can extinguish it. Praise Him! You, beloved Woman Beautiful, are valuable to him and he has much more for you than you may be experiencing.

God is sovereign. He can save people any way he wants to, and he can baptize them with the Holy Spirit any way he wants to. This one thing I know for sure: God is looking for women who thirst for him, who want him in all of his fullness, and who will not limit him because of fear, religious beliefs, ignorance, or because religious leaders and teachers have tried to limit the power of God to the days when Jesus walked the earth. Ladies, it is time to take God out of the box! Will you dare to *believe* that *God is who he says he is* and *he does what he says he will do?*

Don't limit him! Don't be afraid of the changes he wants to bring about in you. He has a beautiful plan for your life. Marlene told me repeatedly over a two-year period, "God's doing an extreme makeover in me." Sometimes, she would tell me through tears of emotional pain. Other times, she would tell me through joyful laughter. I'm having the awesome privilege of watching her beautiful transformation, and she is watching mine. (Our change is still coming and will continue until the day of Christ Jesus.) Don't think this change comes easy. Marlene's extreme makeover has come with a very high price, one many of us will never choose to pay. Yet, she was and is willing to pay the price for a wonderfully intimate fellowship with Holy God. The price of obedience: becoming others-centered, being stretched out of her comfort zone, and giving more of her finances, time, and talents when there appeared to be nothing left to give; the price of praying rather than complaining, the price of praising rather than pouting, the painful price of standing firm in her convictions when collapsing in exhaustion from the spiritual battles would be easier, and the heart-wrenching price of letting go of loved ones when she would rather hold on.

I heard television Bible teacher Andrew Womack say, "I have not arrived yet, but I have left." We, as born-again, spirit-filled Woman Beautifuls, should be able to make the same statement: *I have not arrived yet, but I have left! I am in the process of becoming more like Christ—becoming all he created me to be.* Amen!

Why Obedience?

"It's all about the change. God will not change, conforming to our likeness; therefore we have to change conforming to his." Marlene Mains

Extreme change comes by following the Lord in obedience as he reveals new truths to you. In 1 Samuel 15:22, God makes it very clear that it is better to obey than to sacrifice: "But Samuel replied: 'Does the LORD delight in burnt offerings and sacrifices as much as in obeying the voice of the LORD? To obey is better than sacrifice, and to heed is better than the fat of rams'" (NIV).

Anybody can sacrifice an animal or food or a favorite television show, but it is a much greater expression of love to obey Holy God. What God desires most is our love and devotion, not just a halfhearted sacrifice of whatever it is that we may, on our own, conjure up to give to him. To sacrifice is to make an offering, but to obey is to be an offering. The most powerful and effective form of love we can show God is an obedient heart, mind, and life; not because we have to obey him, but because we want to obey him.

Through deliberate and intentional acts of obedience, the Holy Spirit grows us into the likeness of Christ. His desire for us comes full circle as we choose to obey him one small act of obedience at a time.

Marlene talks about change and changing more than any other woman I know. It is in the changing that we take on the character of Christ. It is the character of Christ that reveals a loving and compassionate God to an unbelieving

world. To obey him is better than sacrifice because it is in the obedience that he is ultimately glorified, and God's glory moves people to want to know him.

The opposite of obedience is, of course, disobedience or rebellion. The first half of 1 Samuel 15:23 says, "For rebellion is as the sin of divination and insubordination is as iniquity and idolatry because you have rejected the word of the Lord."

When a person chooses to rebel against God, she chooses to reject the very word of God. We could spell "word of God" with both a lower case "w" meaning his written word and an upper case "W" meaning the Son of God, who is Jesus Christ. Both acts of rebellion are a serious grievance to God and oneself. It grieves God because, in essence, what is being said and expressed is, "I love myself more than I love you, God," and it's a grievance to the person because God is not obligated to bless rebellion and disobedience. He is only obligated to let the rebellious believer into his heavenly kingdom. Therefore, the disobedient believer does not experience anywhere near the abundant life here on earth that she could would she obey him to the best of her ability.

The abundant life of God I'm talking about is knowing him better and loving him more, hearing his voice and following it, worshiping him with a pure heart, conversing with him regularly, and prospering in the wisdom and understanding of Almighty God. The abundant life knows his heart and mind so intimately that we simply follow in trusting submission.

Not only does obedience change us and bless God,

but it also opens the door wide for us to receive God's blessings. I believe many people want to have fun and enjoy life but think they can't if they live a life wholly committed to Christ; quite the contrary. God desires to pour out on each one of his children so much blessing or abundance that they cannot help but pass the overflow on to others. These blessings include such things as love, peace, joy, health, wealth, friendship, thankfulness, and the list goes on. His greatest joy is prospering you in *every* area of your life, especially your soul. Obeying God brings forth the abundant life he wants all of his children to experience here on earth!

Who said we had to wait until heaven to receive God's best? Not God. Some of his best really can be experienced here in the waiting. And that is his desire for you!

The second half of 1 Samuel 15:23 says, "He has also rejected you from being king." God was speaking specifically to Saul, who had been a rebellious king. He was in the process of dethroning him. If you have placed your trust in Jesus Christ as your Lord and Savior, then you need not worry about God rejecting you as his child. Your eternal position is secure, but you ought not think that you should receive anything more from God. You can expect your blessings in this life to be little to none. You will most likely reap hardship, frustration, and disappointment, and you will live this life constantly striving but never arriving. Not because of God's faithlessness, but because of your disobedience!

Many times, we strive to obey with great diligence, seemingly to no avail. Do not be discouraged! You are in

a pruning process, a process in which you will reap much fruit and great reward if you do not give up. During these times of difficulty, *cry out* to God. You will be amazed at how he moves on your behalf.

The Only Unforgivable Sin

People who seem to have good fortune yet live recklessly, who act mean and cruel and seem to just keep prospering are simply people who know how to manipulate things, people, and circumstances for their own gain. The day will come when they have hell to pay for their disobedience toward God. The disobedience of denying Christ by and through the Holy Spirit is the only unforgivable sin. Yet, this form of obedience is one that so many people claim to have acted on, but their lives say something different.

The word of God says in 2 Timothy 3:5, "There are those holding to a form of godliness yet deny the power (who is the Holy Spirit) thereof. Avoid such men (women) as these." (My emphasis added.) It also says in Luke 12:10, "And everyone who speaks a word against the Son of Man (who is Jesus), it will be forgiven him; but he who blasphemes against the Holy Spirit, it will not be forgiven him." (My emphasis added.) It didn't make sense to me why a person could speak against Christ and be forgiven and yet that same person could speak against the Holy Spirit and not be forgiven. After all, Jesus is the Son of God. Then God revealed to me that it is the Holy Spirit that indwells us, and if we reject the Holy Spirit and his power, then we reject the indwelling; and if we reject the indwelling, then we reject Christ because the Holy Spirit is the person of God who Christ gave in order for us to be born again. If we take on a form of godliness but deny the Holy Spirit who is the "power thereof," then we are rejecting the completion of the plan that God executed through Christ in order to keep us in fellowship with Him even if we sin (See 1 John 2:1, NAS).

Out of the Gutter

"We can take the person out of the gutter, but if we don't take the gutter out of the person, then we have failed." Bill Bright, Founder, Campus Crusades for Christ.

Your spiritual walk with Christ is God's way of taking the gutter out of you. This clean-up work is done through the power of the Holy Spirit as you spend time with God, in his word and prayer as well as with other believers, and as you follow him in obedience.

Will you give God permission to do an extreme makeover in you through his Holy Spirit? God alone is worthy of doing this in you and for you.

Father in heaven, I know that you are all that I need. You are my comforter and my companion. Thank you for sending your Son, Jesus, to die for me. Thank you for drawing me to yourself through him. Thank you for the Holy Spirit, who empowers me to love you and others. I know that he is God with me and in me. He enables me to let go of the past and live

wholly for you in the now. You are my godliness and he is the power thereof.

Thank you for other believers and for women with whom I have a kindred spirit because of our salvation in Christ and because of the filling of the Holy Spirit. Thank you for calling me to yourself and for loving me too much to let me stay the way I was yesterday, last month, and last year. Lord, you amaze me. My desire is to spend time with you each day; both one on one alone time with you, as well as time with you in the fellowship of other believers. Lord, converse with me throughout the day that I will come to know your voice better. Holy God, my desire is to obey you in all that I say and do.

Fill me with your Spirit fresh and new each day that I will glorify your holy name. When I want to be unkind, ungrateful, and pessimistic, remind me that while removing the gutter, there will be many times that giving up and getting even sounds good, but help me recognize the lies of Satan and remain steadfast in your love and faithfulness. May I be aware of your gentle leading at all times. I love you.

You have created me for your good pleasure. Thank you for loving me enough to change me from the inside out. Delight in me as I delight in you. In Jesus' name, I pray. Amen.

Beauty Tips

1. Evaluate what kind of woman you are and what kind you want to be.
2. Determine to spend time with God everyday; preferably first thing each morning.
3. Consider your walk with the Lord: is it a love walk with and for him and others?
4. Ask God to fill you with his Holy Spirit. Thank him for the sealing and praise him for the filling.
5. Invite God to do an extreme makeover in you.
6. Tell Jesus you love him.
7. Tell God you trust him.
8. Practice his presence everyday: praise him with song, listen for his voice, and speak to him as you would a close friend whether you hear him speak back or not.
9. Memorize 1 Peter 1:16.
10. Choose to obey the voice of God.
11. Share your story about receiving Christ as Lord and Savior with someone who needs to hear the truth of Jesus and God's amazing love.
12. Before you attend worship at your home church, spend a few minutes in prayer asking God to prepare your heart to hear him. Turn on Christian music to listen to as you get ready to worship God corporately.

Receiving Jesus as Lord and Savior

God created people because he wanted someone in his likeness that he could have fellowship with, someone he could be intimate with and enjoy, someone who would enjoy him. God wanted a relationship with you.

God is holy. His word tells us that he hates sin. He hates it so much that if we sin it separates us from him. Knowing that we would not be perfect and that we would sin, God executed a plan that would keep us securely in relationship with him even when we failed.

God's plan includes entering into relationship with him through his Son, Jesus Christ.

> All have *sin*ned and *fall short* of the *glory* of God.
>
> Romans 3:23

You don't measure up to God's standard. Nobody does!

> For the *wages* of sin is *death.*
>
> Romans 6:23a

You get paid eternal death, in hell for sinning against God,
But,

> God loved the world so much that He gave His only Son that whoever *believes* in Him will not *perish* but will have *everlasting* life.
>
> John 3:16

Therefore,

> The gift of God is *eternal* life through His Son Jesus Christ.
>
> Romans 6:23b

His gift to you through Jesus is eternal life, in heaven with him.

You see,

> By *grace* you have been saved through *faith* not by yourself, it is the *gift* of God, not of *works* so no one can boast about what he's done in order to enter into heaven.
>
> Ephesians 2:8

It is faith in Jesus Christ that saves you—nothing that you yourself can do.

So,

> If you will confess with your mouth and believe in your heart that Jesus is the Son of God you will be saved.
>
> Romans 10:9

Do you believe in your heart that Jesus is the Son of God, who died for your sins, and that God raised him from the dead?

____

Are you ready to receive Christ as your Savior?

____

Pray this prayer:

God in heaven, thank you for sending your Son to die for me, to free me from the penalty of sin. Lord, please forgive me for sinning against you. At this moment, I am confessing that Jesus is your Son. I believe this in my heart and I know you raised him from the dead. Jesus, come into my heart. Be my Savior and my Lord. Baptize me with your Holy Spirit. I want to live life for you, full of your beauty. In Jesus' name, I pray. Amen.

The angels in heaven are rejoicing over you. Continue reading your Woman Beautiful book to begin growing in your new relationship with Christ. If you don't already, start reading your Bible. Begin in the book of John or the Psalms. Easy to read versions of the Holy Bible are the New American Standard Bible (NASB) or the New International Version (NIV). Find a Bible believing and preaching church and get connected. Tell anyone who will listen what you have just done.

Date I prayed to receive Christ as my Savior and asked him to be my Lord ________________________________

Physical Beauty

“She girds herself with strength and makes her arms strong” (Proverbs 31:17, NAS).

“She knows that taking care of herself is good and she does not entertain idleness” (Proverbs 31: 18).

Step Four

Maintain Your Physical Health

There are many reasons for taking care of your physical body. For one thing, it's the only one you have, and for another it is the temple in which God dwells. The latter truth in itself should move us to take care of our bodies. For many of us, exercise is just one more thing we have to get done in a day. Physical beauty does not begin and end with exercise. It also includes personal hygiene, dress, and diet. Most important to God concerning our bodies is that we take care of them and conduct them in such a way that glorifies him. Praise God, you are Woman Beautiful!

Physical beauty probably demands less time than the other five aspects of beauty. Yet, in one form or another, this aspect of beauty often gets more attention than any other. The word of God says that physical exercise profits a person little. (See 1 Timothy 4:8.) Sadly, for most of us, exercise is a means of maintaining or achieving good looks rather than good health. Exercise or no exercise, everything still goes south; it just moves south a little slower with exercise.

Fortunately, exercise is not the only highway by which we can maintain physical beauty. Other areas of effective maintenance include: muscle tone and strength, proper weight, good blood flow, internal health, hygiene, dress, knowing your body, and sporting a diligent work ethics attitude. These areas of beauty can be achieved and maintained in the convenience of your own home.

Exercise—Don't Cringe. Make It Fun!

A very important part of physical beauty is a personal wellness plan. I encourage every Woman Beautiful to implement a plan that fits her lifestyle.

One day a week, she could work very diligently in her home. Vacuuming, sweeping and mopping, and scrubbing toilets and showers can easily be considered a fitness activity. On other days, Woman Beautiful could turn on her favorite music and dance to it. A consistent twenty-minute fitness activity three times a week is all it takes to achieve and maintain good fitness. After all, most of us are not marathon runners or decathlon enthusiasts. We just want to be able to live our days with reasonable energy and stamina.

What I've learned about myself is that I do not enjoy exercise: especially walking, jogging, and running. Ugh! I will occasionally take a twenty-minute moderate to brisk walk, though it is not my exercise of choice. (Unless, it is with a friend; then it becomes an opportunity of fellowship, and that changes everything.) I spend time each week in some form of body strengthening and stretching simply because I've seen what happens to unused muscles. I do what works for me. Woman Beautiful needs not invest in costly exercise equipment. Items you find in your kitchen

and around your house can get you started. Such things as canned food can be used in place of dumbbells, and furniture can be used as support and even elevation for certain exercises. Check out such magazines as Woman's Day for easy, do at home exercises and fitness suggestions. The 700 Club has a great fitness segment every Wednesday. It also offers free fitness fact sheets that can be yours just by asking. And, Jennifer Brindley, founder of Rise Up Ministry, offers an excellent fitness program that airs on Christian television that is both effective and affordable.

There are lots of ways to burn calories. Did you know that for a woman of my size (5'3.5" and 140 lbs), a three minute kiss burns 2.3 calories? Grocery shopping for one hour burns 233 calories, if I walk and push my shopping cart. Doing laundry for fifteen minutes burns 34 calories. Thirty minutes of snow shoveling burns 194 calories, and one hour of moderate lovemaking burns 104 calories. What is important is that Woman Beautiful does something. Just move it!

But I Like Food!

I like eating. I like the texture, flavor, and smell of food, but that doesn't mean I have to let food control me. Just before I turned forty, I began gaining weight and didn't stop gaining for about three years. Over that three-year span, I gained right at twenty pounds. At my height, 130 pounds is not bad; but 150 pounds is way too heavy. What I have since learned is that all women gain weight during this time period in their lives, and weight loss at age forty and over cannot be done by exercise alone. Woman Beautiful has to take charge of her eating. She cannot eat as much of anything and everything that she wants to. Controlled eating has to be consistent and continued if she wants to lose weight and keep it off. At the writing of this book, I consume on average one meal per day and I try to make that meal one of little consumption.

Simple things like eating smaller portions, not eating in between meals, or better yet eating five really small meals per day, and knocking out drinks that are carbonated and high in sugar and caffeine will slowly drop the weight off of you, and will keep it off of you. Eat with health in mind, not just pleasure or what's most detrimental to Woman Beautiful's body: eating for comfort.

Eating to feel good is almost always why overweight people are overweight. I want to encourage you if you are one who turns to food every time stress takes root, to look to the Savior instead; he will help you feel better, even good. Leave your hurts and disappointments at the foot of the cross and let Jesus bring the sweet relief you need: from the inability to forgive others, tremendous hurt, and agonizing disappointment.

The main eating problems with American people today are that we eat for the wrong reasons and we don't stop until we're stuffed. I can remember the day God revealed this to me about myself. I was crying alligator sized tears in my plate while shoveling the food in. Food does comfort, but it is artificial and temporary comfort at best. If we can determine why we want to eat for comfort, then we can determine to find our comfort in the Lord rather than in

food. Jesus said he would leave the Comforter with us. He has indeed!

Eating to God's Glory

Christ knew when the next bite would be sin. We too are capable of knowing which bite that is. Gluttony is sin that rarely gets mentioned when the typical list of drunkenness, drug addiction, and smoking is spoken of by some religious leaders who are seemingly oblivious to the sin issues that are really holding people in bondage.

There is some speculation as to whether Christ was masculine or handsome or tall. I would say he was probably fit but perfectly average. He knew full well the difference between spiritual strength and stamina and physical strength and stamina; therefore, it is safe to say that he probably didn't spend time building muscle mass. He knew the importance of eating without sinning and maintaining the body by refusing to become idle. Without the convenience of modern refrigeration and ovens, it is very unlikely that he ate more than one meal a day. If he did eat more than once per day, it could have easily been a hearty meal of fresh picked dates or figs and nuts. Because he was Jewish, we can rest assured that he did not partake of anything considered to be non-kosher. A diet full of fish, nuts, and fresh fruit was probably his lifestyle diet; simply average, but healthy. Because he was determined to live a perfect, sinless life, one of the ways he did this was to eat to God's glory, not his own selfish desires. He ate to nourish his physical body, to enjoy fellowship with his followers, and because he, like us, would get hungry. Christ did not eat for any other reason. Had he, he would have been eating in sin.

Did you know that one is considered obese if she is twenty percent heavier than what is considered average for her age and height? For example, at the writing of this book, I am forty-five years old and am 5 feet 3.5 inches tall. I should weigh about 135 pounds. If I weighed 162 pounds, I would be considered obese. It alarms me that a mere twenty-seven pounds moves me from simply being a little overweight to being obese. I've seen me at 150 pounds, and believe me, I would be considered by many as being obese wearing an additional 12 pounds. That number alarms me because "overweight" seems to be a very accepted and approved fad in the United States right now. For the pure health of it, we should be less approving and more preventing. It is vital that we understand how being overweight reveals two things: we are not eating to God's glory, and we have issues that need to be dealt with.

Fasting and Prayer

Spend time in fasting and prayer. I am not suggesting that you fast in order to lose weight. You fast in order to prepare your heart and mind to hear from the Lord. But what I have found in fasting is this: when I deny myself food and focus intentionally on the Lord, he energizes me. Without exception, I feel better physically as well as mentally, emotionally, and spiritually when I am going without bread and am being fed by the Lord. Wonderful changes take place in me. I love the way I feel, the attitude I sport, and the spiritual insights God gives me. I can look at people through the eyes of Christ easier, and stepping into the presence of God becomes almost effortless.

Weight loss is an added result of fasting, and better eating habits are a direct result of submitting to the Lord. Woman Beautiful cannot fast and pray without benefiting mentally, emotionally, spiritually, and physically.

The book of Daniel is an amazing account of God's faithfulness to a man who would rather die than disobey his God. This written account of God's goodness convinces a believer in the importance of fasting and prayer. Daniel's reward came in the physical, mental, emotional, and spiritual realms. Fasting with prayer is the most vital habit you can establish for the good and prosperous health of your total being.

In Ezekiel 4:4, God commanded him to bear the iniquities of Israel. During the time Ezekiel was to bear these sins, by lying on his side one day for each year of Israel's iniquity, God told him exactly what he was to eat and drink and how often he was to partake of his supplemental food and water. God instructed Ezekiel to make bread consisting of wheat, barley, lentils, millet, and spelt.

As unappetizing as the bread described here sounds, it was the exact supplement that Ezekiel needed to sustain him while he was bearing the sins of Israel—which in reality was an extended fast from food while lying on his side. The amount of bread that Ezekiel was to eat was 20 shekels a day, or about 12 ounces a day by today's measure.

God instructed him to eat the bread from "time to time" or as we might say it, "eat five small meals a day."

The water he was to drink was the sixth part of one hin, or by today's measure, 96 ounces. Is this diet beginning to sound familiar? Isn't it amazing that God prescribed for Ezekiel what dieticians, doctors, and other health enthusiasts prescribe for good eating habits today: five small meals and twelve 8 oz. glasses of water a day. Ezekiel did not die, but was adequately sustained during this time of extended fasting (Ezekiel 4:9). Please note that these figures are based on available information and are not intended to be absolutely, mathematically precise. But rather, an excellent guide by which you can use to maintain a well-balanced diet of food intake. What you need to realize is that you can live on a lot less food then the average American consumes daily. If you're following the Woman Beautiful format, then you have been fasting once a week from evening meal to evening meal. Ask the Lord to help you continue a lifestyle of denying yourself (fasting from food) and partaking of him (prayer and Bible study). Ask him to make you sensitive to the times he leads you to fast and pray.

Take Vitamin Supplements

These three vitamins are recommended by specialists almost unanimously: Vitamin E, Beta Carotene, and Vitamin C. If you don't take anything else, take these. Vitamin E contributes to cardiovascular, mental, and (in men) prostate health. Make sure you are not taking a

synthetic Vitamin E. Look at the back label. It will either say d or dl; dl means it is a synthetic vitamin. Look for the d only. Beta Carotene is a powerful antioxidant that helps your body flush impurities, and Vitamin C helps boost your immune system. My husband and I also take Vitamin B-6, which is good for joints and in many people will aid in preventing/stopping carpal tunnel; B-12 sublingual, which boosts metabolism and nervous system health; and we take fish oil, which is high in omega-3 fatty acids, which helps maintain heart, vascular, and mental health. We also take Co-Q10, which is good for your heart, eyes, arteries, lungs, skin, and more.

I cannot take a multi-vitamin because it nauseates me. Therefore, I take these individual vitamins each day. Be sure to take the recommended dose. If you are in serious lack of certain vitamins, seek guidance from a professional who can wisely guide you in changing the dosage. You can find good, affordable vitamins at your local "everything store" and at health food stores. I highly recommend that you purchase, read, and apply The Maker's Diet by Dr. Jordan Rubin. You will be enlightened and blessed in the understanding of the physical you that God created. You will not only feel healthy but will become healthy. Don't get caught up in the inability to find organic milk and cheese or vegetables; what is important is that you apply what you can to your daily diet.

Please note that we are all on a diet. Your daily food intake is your daily diet. One woman's diet may be a regular consumption of pizza and cheeseburgers with French fries while another woman's diet consists of fresh garden salads with lean cuts of beef or grilled chicken breasts. What probably needs to take place, in many Woman Beautifuls, is a changed diet.

Personal Hygiene

When I think of hygiene, I sometimes suggest to God that he could have caused me to be born during a time when taking a bath was an acceptable weekly occurrence. It seems to be time that I could better use doing something else. So, for Woman Beautiful who suffers from the same "Do I have to take a shower?" dilemma that I do, here we go.

Shower or bathe at least every other day. For some, this is a no-brainer. But for others, you know exactly what I am saying. You may need to ask the neighbor lady or your best girl friend to come over to watch the kids while you shower and dress for the day. But do it! This could very easily be your quiet spot for the day—time to think, pray, or even cry. A little bit of pampering yourself can go a long way, especially if you only shower every other day.

Showering immediately after the kids are in bed is a perfect way to relax and wash away the stresses of the day. It also leaves a clean and comfy body for bedtime. I know you're tired at the end of the day and you still have work to be done, but stop everything and douse yourself with a little TLC.

Do your hair and makeup every day. If you don't wear makeup, then be sure to moisturize. This makes you feel good and gets you ready for whatever the day may hold,

and your husband and children will be proud to call you theirs.

A makeup must if you wear makeup: never just wear concealer or foundation. It really makes a woman look sickly—although there is a mineral based powder foundation available that gives skin a beautiful glow that can be worn with little other makeup. Still, be sure to wear a light lip-gloss with it.

If you're of a denomination that prohibits the wearing of makeup, then be sure to use a nice moisturizer. You will be surprised at the clean, fresh glow it gives you.

This is my personal routine:

1. Moisturize with Olay
2. Apply foundation
3. Apply translucent powder to entire face
4. Apply powder blush
5. Outline lips
6. Outline eyes with soft eyeliner, and then smudge eyeliner lines to soften the eyes
7. Apply mascara
8. Brush up eyebrows, apply brow liner, and brush eyebrows again to soften the brow line
9. Apply lipstick

My daily routine takes all of seven minutes. Woohoo!

Be sure to wear makeup that complements your skin tone. If you're not sure of what products to buy, it would be worth it to pay for a makeup facial or to schedule one at a local department store (they sometimes do them free if you buy the makeup there). Be careful not to purchase more than you need. If you're not used to wearing makeup, do not let the clinician talk you into a bunch of gaudy stuff that will make you feel like "Loosie Susie."

I contacted a makeup clinician from a well-known makeup company in order to get a blonde eyebrow pencil. I knew the company carried the exact color I needed. I told her exactly what I wanted and wondered could she still get it for me. With a free cleansing consultation, she would be glad to get me one. I scheduled an appointment, excited about finally getting the eyebrow pencil that I knew would be perfect. I went to my appointment. I eventually left there, an hour later, with 170 dollars less than when I entered her home—and with no eyebrow pencil. Needless to say, I did not go back. I still get my eyebrow pencil from the company, but from a different clinician. She delights in my little order and very politely says, "Is there anything else you need today?"

Dressed as a Daughter of the King

Wear clothes that fit you and that are comfortable. I'm not suggesting sweat pants and t-shirts! Clothes that fit well, look nice, and feel good on should be a daily dress. We as Christian women need to look appealing to the women of the lost world. Who wants to listen to us if we, as my momma would say, "Look like an unmade bed"? We are representatives of Holy God. We need to look well-kept.

To the best of your ability, wear clothes that are well

laundered. I am fanatical about little, including my clothes, yet I do believe that clothing should be clean and wrinkle free—at least when you put them on. Christian women are a replica of the holy and living God. Their dress should reflect his adorning. If you're wearing clothes covered in animal hair and severely wrinkled, you should not be surprised when others, less emotionally and spiritually mature, don't invite you to have lunch with them or participate in events which include their peers. You might have a personality like none other, or you may be a wealth of information, but physical appearance is a barricade for many. So be mindful and careful about the laundering of your clothing. I know this sounds shallow and it is, but most of the people in the world base their willingness to "give somebody a chance" or to "get to know somebody" by the way they look. You, Woman Beautiful, need to look like a child of the King. You have a message people want and need to hear. Your clean and orderly physical appearance is important to the way people will perceive you as well as receive you.

You may enjoy shopping at secondhand stores; many women do. I myself have shopped at secondhand stores and still do on occasion. I only have one comment to make: just because you shop at a secondhand store doesn't mean you have to look like it! If you're lacking in wardrobe coordinating skills, ask a woman from your church to give you some helpful hints on how to put together a secondhand wardrobe. It is the same as if you shopped at Neiman Marcus or Saks Fifth Avenue. One of the best-dressed women I know does all of her shopping at secondhand stores. She always looks very nice and even stylish. Another woman I remember crossing paths with was a guest speaker at our MOPS group many years ago. She was adorable from head to toe—coordinated from the earrings to the shoes. After many of us had commented on her very attractive outfit, she delightfully bragged about her blouse and skirt that she had purchased at the Salvation Army. So remember, just because you enjoy buying used clothing doesn't mean you have to look like you shop at the local secondhand store.

What about My Body Parts?

Don't try to disguise your body parts, but don't try to accentuate them either. My friend Paula is the one who said, "I've finally decided that my boobs are going to stick out and there is nothing I can do about it." Buy clothes that fit not just your boobs but also your shoulders and arm length, and not just your behind but also your waist and leg length. When shopping, don't expect a sales clerk to be totally honest about the way the clothes you're trying on fit you. The sales clerk is in it for the money. When shopping, take a friend along that will be honest with you. Don't buy anything that you don't love, feel good in, and will enjoy wearing, and don't buy anything that doesn't fit well at the time of the purchase.

My Husband, My Lover—

Part of My Physical Wellness Plan

Enjoy regular bedroom fellowship with your husband: two or more times a week, except when you are menstruating or have agreed to a time of fasting and prayer. It's amazing what burns calories and gets the heart pumping. Remember, one hour of moderate lovemaking burns 104 calories. Woohoo! Bedroom fellowship is good for your husband's heart too, in both health and happiness. Did I mention he burns calories during moderate lovemaking also?

As part of your overall wellness, bedroom fellowship should be partaken of regularly. It is good for the emotions as well as for the heart, literally. During lovemaking a healthy adrenalin is produced that is good for the heart and circulatory system. Our Creator had more in mind for man and wife when he gave us the gift of lovemaking than we realize. Babies are not the only positive fruit birthed out of our expression of love for one another; there can and should be mental and emotional security, reconciliation, forgiveness, bonding, unity, and a mutual tenderness toward one another that stems out of the physical aspect of our physical, one flesh relationship. All of which promote good physical health.

My Body Is Fallen, My God Is Not!

Know your body! It is very important to know your cycle. Hormones play an enormous part in our attitudes.

Know your cycle! You can take preventative measures to combat emotional irritability and physical fatigue. I heard Kathy Troccoli say about herself, "I have one good week a month." I was elated! There was another woman out there who knew her body. What I have also come to understand is that out of that one good week I have two really good days. Ladies, do you understand what we are up against? We live in fallen bodies, but we do not serve a fallen God. Hallelujah! Through Christ Jesus, we have victory and authority over this body. It is vital that you know your body and that you help your daughters and daughters-in-law know their bodies also. Woman Beautiful, you can settle for the ups and downs of Ovulation S, (that time of the month when you are ovulating, which can be just as hormonally unbalanced as the rest of your monthly cycle), PMS, and post-MS, or you can take authority over your fallen body by praying, trusting God, and making preventative changes. Once you have determined victory, you must expect positive results.

Listed are the changes I began making, and it didn't take long for me to start seeing results:

1. The first thing I did was admit to God and myself that my body was fallen but that he was not. Even though PMS plagued me each month, I had power for victory should I choose to walk in it.

2. I began to pray, asking God to help me identify the symptoms and then give me wisdom on how to combat those symptoms.

3. I quit drinking caffeine and Pepsi (my pop of choice) and lowered my overall carbonated soda intake to

less than one a week (believe me; this was only at the Lord's instruction).

4. I began going to bed earlier, especially during the week before my period.
5. I began changing my daily eating habits, which consisted of less processed food, less junk food, and more fruits and veggies as well as eating smaller portions.
6. I learned to recognize the little annoyances that really bugged me during PMS, and I started walking away from those petty situations that could easily turn into full-blown arguments. (Especially with my teenage daughters who might also be suffering from PMS.)

   If necessary, I would take over the counter medication for headaches, water retention, and fatigue.
7. Rest. Going to bed by 10:00 p.m. or shortly thereafter is one of the absolute best things I can do. Plenty of rest is vital to my total being.
8. Most importantly, I began thanking God every month for delivering me from the bondage of PMS, which could very easily be hurtful to my most important relationships—those with my husband and children.

I encourage you, Woman Beautiful, to pay attention to your cycle for three months. Mark *each* day with a simple face (any calendar will do): a smiley face for a really good day, a straight-mouthed face for an okay day, a frowning face for a bad day, and a frowning face with a cloud hanging over it for a really bad day. You will be gauging your physical, mental, and emotional fatigue—as well as headaches, sleeplessness, hunger cravings, irritability, and constipation. You may also experience breast tenderness and swelling, as well as swelling of the whole body and perhaps an increase or decrease in sex drive.

The looming cloud of oppression can be combated with prayer, soothing music, and some quiet time away from the busyness of life.

If you struggle with depression, you will still be able to gauge the effects of your hormones. Thankfully, antidepressants help with the down times of PMS. If you are on medication for depression, do not hit and miss taking it. It will help keep you mentally and emotionally balanced during PMS. If you quit taking your depression medicine, you will more than likely become even more oppressed and depressed feeling than with your medication. Be sure to take your medication just as the doctor prescribed it.

Try to keep your PMS days as stress free as possible. Do whatever it takes to avoid "nit-picky" quarreling that leads only to arguments. Plan ahead for these days; cook stress-free meals, even if it means supper will be coming out of a box. Talk to your husband about the four to seven days prior to your period, expressing your need for a little extra grace and help. Take your thoughts captive. I began reminding myself that *I am suffering from PMS and things really aren't quite as big as my mind seems to be making them* and *all will be better in a few days.*

The word says that, "All things work together for the good for those who love Him and are called according to His purpose" (Romans 8:28), and I believe that firmly! If it weren't for PMS, I may have gone through life letting the inappropriate behavior of others just roll off my back. But because the difficulties of life were amplified during certain times of the month, it moved me to cry out to God and seek his help, healing, and change in others but especially in myself. There's not too much worse than acting like an idiot rather than a loving wife, mom, or friend.

Change in herself is what every Woman Beautiful needs; whether she wants to admit it or not. Take advantage of every opportunity to understand yourself a little bit better; know what makes you tick, what makes you sick, and what moves you closer to God.

I believe balance, under the leadership of Holy God, is the key to successful living, even when one's hormones are raging! Woman Beautiful, you go girl!

Lord, you are more amazing than I can really fathom. I believe that you are the help that I need to accept the physical that I am but to press on toward the physical you created me to be. Father, help me forgive those who've hurt me so that I will eat because I'm hungry and not because I'm angry or wounded. Teach me to eat in a way that is most beneficial to my physical well-being. Lead me in fasting and praying that I will experience you in extreme ways. Holy Spirit, teach me to choose clothes that look good, feel good, and that I will best represent you in. When I feel like being idle, energize me so that I will burn calories as I productively carry out your kingdom work. Convince me that I have authority over my body because you are not fallen; enable me to make necessary changes as I rely fully on you. Remind me to initiate lovemaking with my husband because it stimulates good health for both of us—individually and in our marriage. Move me to dress for the day even when I don't feel like it. Father, more than anything I want to live out this life in a way that is pleasing to you. In Jesus' name, I pray. Amen.

Beauty Tips

1. Spend twenty minutes in exercise three days a week.
2. Work at losing the extra weight you may be carrying around.
3. Spend time in fasting and prayer each week.
4. Take vitamin supplements and drink twelve 8 oz. glasses of water a day. (You can drink small glasses of water faster than you can drink large glasses.)
5. Shower or bathe, at the very least, every other day.
6. Attend to your physical appearance everyday.
7. Wear clothes that fit, are comfortable, clean, and wrinkle free.
8. Enjoy regular bedroom fellowship with your husband.
9. Know your body. (What happens mentally, emotionally, and physically throughout your menstrual cycle?) If you are in menopause, you too are experiencing hormonal changes that affect your mental, emotional and physical health; you are still in need of knowing your body.
10. Work diligently at all you do and then rest.

Financial Beauty

“She shops wisely” (Proverbs 31:13*).*

“She invests her money wisely” (Proverbs 31:16*).*

“She extends her hand to the poor and she stretches out her hands to the needy” (Proverbs 31:20, NAS).

“She uses her time and talents to generate money for the household” (Proverbs 31:24*).*

“*She takes good care of her household* and does not eat the bread of idleness” (Proverbs 31:27, NAS).

Step Five

Become a Good Steward of the Money Entrusted to You

Financial beauty has definitely been my most difficult challenge in the Woman Beautiful process. As much as I wanted to be pleasing and obedient to God and pleasing and submissive to my husband, nothing seemed to take root in my heart and mind in the area of financial stewardship. That is until I opened my eyes one day and realized I had managed to incur twenty thousand dollars worth of credit card debt. I am embarrassed to confess that enormous amount. The guilt and shame did not compare, though, to the brokenness I felt between God and me, and most certainly between John and me.

John knew I had debt, yet he had no idea as to how much. I had this deep, dark secret that hung, looming heavily, over my head day after day. I remember asking the Lord to tell John how much debt I had so that I would not have to. Sometimes, though, we just have to walk through the muck and mire as part of our beauty process. Telling John was most definitely muck and mire. I dreaded that more than anything I'd had to confess to him thus far.

God's Faithfulness

I began asking God for direction in order to pay off my debt. The very first thing God told me to do was to obey John. Even though John didn't give the way I wanted him to give, he did have excellent moneysaving and debt-eliminating skills that I needed to possess. So I became a student of my husband in the area of money, not only a student of my husband but also of financially successful people.

John's first priority has always been to save, save, *save!* So that's where I began. You're probably wondering why I didn't start with tithing; tithing is something I had trouble with from the time John and I married. I had very little personal income, and even though I did have control over John's salary check, he did not want me tithing. As much as I wanted to tithe, as much as I knew to tithe, and as much as I wanted to bless God by tithing, I still struggled with submitting to John and obeying God until one day during my personal quiet time. I was conversing with God over debt, tithing, saving, and being a good steward of God's estate in general. Here is our dialogue:

"Father, John says it's his responsibility to tithe the salary check. What do you think about that?" (At that time, John admitted that he was not tithing the salary check, only his commission checks.)

"Obey your husband."

"Okay, but Lord you know I want to give. What about my income? How should I give out of it?"

"Give what I tell you to give."

"That's easy. Okay."

Woman Beautiful, this was a morning of divine revelation as well as revolution! I had finally been freed from years of struggling with obeying God and submitting to my husband. (Another one of those submitting in rebellion things.) Let me tell you that God never has me give less than ten percent. In fact, he almost always has me give more than ten percent. God made it very clear that morning that John was indeed the *spiritual leader* of our home, and under that title, John would be accountable to God as to whether or not the salary check was tithed. I simply had to obey.

"Why did I have to *obey* John?" you might ask. At that point in my walk, I was not yet willing to peacefully submit to John's unwillingness to approve of my tithing and giving. John would not allow me to tithe or give, especially if it wasn't his idea. That, beloved Woman Beautiful, was a control issue for me and I, like many of you, have no desire to be controlled. Even though God owns it all, in John's eyes, John owns it all, and I had to submit to John's headship.

Debt Retirement

I had gotten into so much debt trying to make a business work that every time my husband asked about my debt all I could say was, "A lot; I have a lot of debt." Never before had I been ashamed of debt, but this time was different. My debt teetered right at twenty thousand, and I could not tell my husband. Remorse, regret, shame, and fear hung over my head for many months that quickly turned into years. I knew what caused debt and how to avoid it, and although my spending habits had changed, I still struggled with the desire to receive John's approval in the area of finances. Money had always been a major issue between us and I wanted to show him that I could be a financial contributor and not a financial casualty in our marriage. So I signed on with a major home decorating company and started spending money in order to make money. The only problem was, the money I was spending was plastic, and as the weeks passed I went further and further into debt. Three years later and with a ton of debt, I went to the Lord and told him I was done; I couldn't do it any more.

The day I told God that I was done trying to make money so John would hopefully approve of me, he simply responded, "Finally." It seems like the Lord went to work in me immediately. This ugly monster I had entangled myself with would not be turned loose by any means other than God. I began crying out to him for help. I had no job and a mountain of debt. My monthly payments were in excess of six hundred dollars. I eventually fell behind on my payments, and before long creditors were ringing my phone several times a day. This period in my life became darker each time the phone rang. Then one day, broken before the Lord, I told him he had to help me because I could not make the payments. On that day, he told me he would pay off my debt in a lump sum. I believed him!

Even though the Lord told me he would pay off my debt in a lump sum, I had to make the monthly payments until then. In my financial beauty process, I knew that it was not John's responsibility to pay off my debt. The debt was in my name alone and was not approved by him. So there I was, buried in debt with little to no personal income. This Woman Beautiful has taken a fresh and deeper faith in God in which I am truly delighting.

The first thing I did was to call a consumer credit counseling company. They consolidated some of my debt and lowered my monthly payment. The pay off dropped from twenty-five years to five years. Two months prior to making that call, I had determined that I would no longer take money out of the household account to pay off my debt; therefore, I had fallen behind on my monthly payments. They assured me they would recoup any late fees and over the limit fees that I had incurred, which would lower my outstanding balance. Because the debt was in my name, John's credit would not be affected. The monthly payments would be drafted directly from my checking account, and I could raise the payment, change the draft date if I needed to, and even say toward what credit card I wanted any extra payment amount to go to. It was still my debt and I still had some control over the management of it, but I decided to let them do their job. Upon hanging up the phone I thanked the Lord and could finally see a very dim light at the end of my really long tunnel.

Still No Income

After about three months of falling behind on credit card debt payments, because I would not make the payments out of the household account, I began earnestly seeking the Lord for employment. I needed something that would allow me to continue home schooling our daughters yet pay enough to make my monthly credit card payments. Each day, I began reading the "help wanted" ads in our local newspaper. One day, I came upon an ad that needed someone to work Monday through Friday, afternoons only. The ad requested someone with experience in legal secretarial skills. I thought to myself, *Why not apply?* I only needed to send my resume to a blind box, and though I had never written a resume, nor did I have any legal assistant experience, I knew I served a very capable God.

A few days later, the phone rang and it was the law firm. I went in for an interview, and when it was over I felt very confident I would be offered the position. The head legal assistant assured me she would contact me by Wednesday of the next week. The next day, I began questioning what the Lord was capable of doing, and those doubtful thoughts permeated my heart and mind: *You're not really trusting the Lord to pay off your debt in a lump sum. You can't home school and work. You won't be able to spend time with your grandbabies.* I began telling the Lord I didn't want the job. Wednesday came and went, and I had heard nothing from the firm. I was somewhat relieved, but by Friday I had flip-flopped back to wanting the job. So on Friday afternoon, I made a call to the firm. The secretary told me that they had decided on someone whom they felt was better qualified. Disappointment sunk in, but more than that I was grieved that I hadn't trusted God to do what I'd asked; provide me with a job that would cover my monthly debt payments and allow me to take care of my family. I asked his forgiveness and prayed that he would reopen that door. A week later the phone rang and it was the law firm. The secretary told me the girl they hired didn't work out and would I still be interested in coming to work for the firm. Wow! I was amazed at God's faithfulness.

The firm started me at eight dollars an hour with a promise of a review and pay raise at the end of ninety days. My work responsibilities included answering the phone, filing, running errands, watering the plants, and other such tasks that were menial but needed. My attitude was "do all things as unto God, not unto man." By the end of my third week, Delia, the head secretary, came to me and said, "We're going to give you a raise; starting with this pay period, you'll be making ten dollars an hour." Woohoo! God is faithful.

At the end of my third month with the firm, the morning girl announced she would be quitting. They offered me the opportunity to work as many more hours as I would like; more of God's faithfulness. I presented the firm with an hourly plan that would work for me and one with the intentions of going full-time on September first. They accepted my offer, and my debt began coming down. Not only was it coming down, but also, by God's goodness, I was making the monthly payments out of my own hard-earned money.

Prior to that, not a day went by where I didn't have a gut-ache because of my inexcusable debt, yet great joy filled my soul because God had provided a way where there seemed to be no way out of it. Whenever asked where I worked, many people would say, "Oh, are you a legal secretary?" Without hesitation, my response would be, "No. I'm the head gofer girl." And the Lord knows I was thankful for it!

Woman Beautiful While at Work

I had been working on the Woman Beautiful series since the spring of 2004, and with the permission of my boss, I started taking my personal writing files to the office; in my free time I was able to work very diligently at completing *Woman Beautiful.* God *is* the God of provision. If you will get out of his way, he will do great and mighty things on your behalf too.

Tithing

Understanding the tithe and first fruits creates an eagerness to give according to God's commands. Because he owns it all, a person is to give in agreement with his standards and expectations, not according to "her own" understanding. I once heard a well-known money advisor say that there are times when we get ourselves into such a financial bind that we cannot tithe. I am in total disagreement with that comment. Nowhere in Scripture does it say that we can give a little until we can give more. Scripture is very clear on giving the full tithe.

Before you argue that the New Testament doesn't talk about tithing, be reminded of Malachi 3:6, where God himself says, "For I, the LORD, do not change ... " Because he is the God who does not change, it is safe to say that his command on tithing has never changed either. If that

is not enough, then read Luke 18:12 as a Pharisee prays, "I fast twice a week; I pay tithes of all that I get," and Jesus' own words to the Pharisees in Matthew 23:23: "Woe to you, scribes and Pharisees, hypocrites! For you tithe mint and dill and cumin, and have neglected the weightier provisions of the law: justice and mercy and faithfulness; but these are the things you should have done without neglecting the others (tithing)" (my emphasis added). The Pharisees and scribes did right in tithing, but Jesus commended them as being things they *should have done* without neglecting the other important acts of serving the Lord.

Tithe literally means "a tenth part of." Whereas first fruits means "the first part of." In the biblical reference to the tithe, we are commanded to give the first tenth of all of our increase: before we pay our bills; before we buy our groceries; before we buy our medication; before we pay the babysitter; before we buy that pair of shoes we just can't live without. The tithe comes out first! And it is always to be, at the very least, one tenth of our total increase.

Taxes vs. Tithe

Many people get caught up in an age-old question, "Do I tithe the gross or net income?" At which amount you tithe, in my opinion, is personal preference. When being questioned about paying taxes Jesus said, "Then give to Caesar the things that are Caesar's and to God the things that are God's" (See Luke 20:23–25, NAS). Unlike Mark 12:30 and 31, when asked about the greatest command Jesus replied, "'Love the Lord your God with all your heart and with all your soul and with all your mind and with all your strength.' The second is this: 'Love your neighbor as yourself.'" The command to love places God in the first or highest place of love. When we do love God first, it becomes easier to love others the way he wants us to. But in reference to giving, God tells us to give to Caesar what he has demanded and then, give to God what he has commanded.

There is a difference between the government's demand and God's command. Greed would create a need that the government would have to demand taxes, as a *willful* contribution. This willful contribution is punishable by law if a person doesn't willfully pay it. But God's command is offered to his children as a request of the heart. His desired result is loving, willful obedience.

The tax has never been considered "gain" because the government demands that it, the tax, be given to it, the government. This releases us from the dilemma of what has plagued many of us since taxes were first administered and has probably prevented us from giving joyfully. Either way is acceptable unto God and brings glory to him. What is important is that we give from the first of our gain. At whatever line you want to call gain; then let it so be. Don't "not give," and don't be dismayed because you are torn between gross and net; another lie from Satan that God's people have got to recognize and overcome. Many believers tithe the gross and then tithe the tax return. These people know full well that they cannot out give God, but they sure have fun trying!

Obedient tithing is vital to our financial blessing. The

word of God says, "Give and it shall be given to you. They will pour into your lap in good measure—pressed down, shaken together and running over. For by your standard of measure it will be measured to you in return" (Luke 6:38, NAS).

As the fields of the Old Testament were harvested, field owners were commanded to leave the corners uncut and to let any dropped grain lay so that the poor, widows, and aliens (foreigners in the country) could come and gather what had been left behind. Those doing the gleaning would press the grains into their basket and shake it in an effort to fit as much into the basket as possible. The poor would not be able to glean the fields again until next harvest. They would press and shake and press and shake until the basket was running over. That is exactly how God wants to give to his obedient children: pressed down, shaken together, and running over. Hallelujah!

Offerings—Sheer Pleasure

Giving the offering is one of the most pleasurable and spiritually maturing acts of obedience we can participate in. God stretches us as he leads us in the giving of offerings. The offering is an obedient act of the will that asks God what to give and then does as he says. This is where he completely separates those who give begrudgingly from those who give joyfully in an effort to show love: love for God, love for his kingdom and kingdom work, and love for his creation—people. To tithe is to say, "I will obey you." But to make offerings is to say, *All I have really does belong to you, Lord. I love you and will obey you. I will give as you lead me to give.* Tithing requires no prayer, only the ability to calculate ten percent. Offerings, on the other hand, require asking, listening, and obeying. Sometimes giving an offering only requires hearing and obeying. That, beloved Woman Beautiful, is the greatest act of monetary offering you will ever do. When God says, "I want you to give five hundred dollars to such and such ministry," your only response should be, "Okay." Do as he says and get ready for an outpouring.

I remember the day God told me to give away the greeting cards I design. I had every reason imaginable for not obeying: the expense of having them printed, the hours I put into each card, the expense of having them printed, my desire to make money, and the expense of having them printed. A friend finally said something that changed my attitude about giving away my cards. He said, "Amanda, God wants you to give your cards away because he wants to bless your obedience." I am more convinced now than ever before, when God says, "Give it away," it's because he has some kind of really big blessing in store for you.

In early 2008, the Lord told my husband to give some large expensive equipment to a disaster relief team we had some affiliation with. When John told me what the Lord had said, my only response was, "Honey, if the Lord said give it, you need to give it because he wants to bless you even more." John obeyed, and God's blessings continually increase.

God Blesses Obedience

The word says, "… has the Lord as much delight in burnt offerings and sacrifices as in obeying the voice of the Lord? Behold, to obey is better than sacrifice, and to heed than the fat of rams" (1 Samuel 15:22, NAS). If your giving is a sacrificial act of obedience, you will be pleasing to God and he will honor your obedience. Most offerings will be somewhat sacrificial. That is why the obedience is so honoring to God. If you recall the widow's mite in Mark 12:41–44, she not only gave her tithe, but also her offering. She threw in everything that she had, not just 10 percent and a little offering, but all that she had. Her sacrificial offering pleased the Lord so much she is still spoken of today. We are not told just how much God gave back to her, but we can be sure it was a lot more than she threw in.

Malachi 3 makes it clear how we are to give the tithe, where we are to give the tithe, and what we can expect in return. God spoke the truth to his people when they asked, "How have we robbed you?" His reply? "In tithes and offerings." He then implored them to give the full tithe and then added, "Test me now in this and see if I will not open for you the windows of heaven and pour out for you a blessing until it overflows." Woman Beautiful, you should be compelled to take the tithe challenge! Give your tithe joyfully, make your offerings of love, and watch what God will do. He is not a liar. He will not change his mind. And you cannot out give him. Try it!

Back to Saving

God told me to begin saving twenty-five percent of the salary check. I was to put 12.5 percent into our long-term mutual fund savings (which at John's insistence, I had already been doing for about a year) and 12.5 percent into our short-term savings at our local bank. The mapped out plan of action God began to take me on became more exciting each day.

I began searching money saving/growing options such as CDs, mutual funds, regular savings accounts, and money market accounts. After researching many options, I decided to invest with an online investment company that allowed me to start with an amount that fit my budget. It kept my money accessible if need be, but also motivated me to leave it alone to let it grow. My steps were only baby steps, but they were exciting. My first goal was to save five hundred dollars in my short-term savings account at our local bank. Afterwards, I would invest one half of my 12.5 percent in my savings account and the other half in my online investment account. John always says, "You're not making money unless you're making it while you're asleep." I'm having fun making money while I'm sleeping!

You Have to Save in Order to Give!

Marlene and God were my only confidants during the beginning of my debt realization. The word of God says, "We are to confess our sins one to another that we would be healed" (James 5:16). Confessing my debt and what

got me in debt, even to Marlene, was difficult, but when I began to confess my sin of disobedience, God began to work a whole new work in me. I was being healed of the financially based sin that had plagued me for so long.

In expressing my desire to give and give big, my friend simply said, "You have to save in order to give." That one little statement blew me away. Why would I expect God to provide extra money for me to give to those in need or to his kingdom work if he had provided plenty and I carelessly squandered it?

God Owns It All; I Am Simply His Manager

My sin issue was not that I was a poor money manager plagued by a generational curse, but that I refused to surrender to God as the owner of all things. Understanding generational curses and how they affect us enables us to confront the problem head-on and make necessary changes under the power of the Holy Spirit. A person has to not only acknowledge God as the owner of the earth and all that is in it, but she *must also* surrender to his ownership. I remember listening to a CD in which the speaker told me to walk into my house, look around, and say out loud, "It's not mine; it all belongs to God;" to look into my wallet or check book and say, "It's not mine; it all belongs to God;" to get into my vehicle and say, "It's not mine; it belongs to God." For several weeks, I did just that. I still do if I try to do my own thing with God's estate.

There is one thing God had to reveal to me in the ownership realm: in John's eyes, he owned the salary check, and I was to manage it for him. Woman Beautiful, I don't know how you and your husband manage your household income, but I do know this, God owns it all and he has made your husband chief executive officer over your household, including the money in it. Therefore, your husband has to manage it like he owns the piece of God's estate entrusted to him. We all know that the owner of anything treats it better than the hired hand. I had to begin treating our finances with respect toward John, which ultimately pleased and glorified God.

Your husband, perhaps like mine, has made you managing officer over some of your household income or maybe all of it. You, beloved Woman Beautiful, must obey your husband. Now don't be confused, if your husband has zero money management skills, don't squander your household money. Grow in the wisdom of Holy God and let him lead you in a good stewardship plan. You can do this by seeking wise Christian counseling in the area of money management. Good books along with study guides are available to help you. Dave Ramsey's *Financial Peace University* is an excellent place to start learning to be the best steward you can be.

I have learned to follow this simple guide: bring the full tithe into the store house (ten percent), and then pay yourself twenty percent. By paying yourself, I mean save. (I save twenty-five percent because financially, I can.) Your twenty percent is not to blow but to save. Put ten percent into long-term savings and ten percent into short-term savings. (Short-term meaning money you can easily access if you have an emergency.) With consistent contributions to your savings, this works great.

"What about me?" you might be saying. You get 10 percent of what is left over after the bills, groceries, and other necessary expenses have been paid. If there is twenty dollars left over, you get two dollars and the rest goes into a miscellaneous expense account that is used for bread, milk, stamps, and anything else that may come up where you need just a little extra money. Don't worry, you will not have to go without for long. You will soon be growing money in your long-term savings account, your short-term savings account, and your miscellaneous account. The key to growing your miscellaneous account is to not spend it just because it's there. When a need or want (within reason) arises, you will have money readily available.

My husband expects me to save lots of money, pay whatever bills I may have, spend lots of money, and never run out of cash. This, Woman Beautiful, is impossible for most of us. I save lots of money, pay whatever bills I may have, spend very little money, and always, always seem to run out of cash and out of money in my checking account. Interestingly, John asked me this question: "How wealthy do you want to be?" I had to think on that awhile. Finally, I was able to answer him: 1) wealthy enough to give one hundred thousand dollars a year in tithes, offerings, and help to others without affecting my savings; and, 2) wealthy enough that no matter what John decides to do with money, whether in business or personally, it will not affect the money I have access to. How wealthy is that?

In regards to number two listed above: if you've ever

been through Financial Peace University, you know exactly what Dave Ramsey's wife meant when she said, "I can buy groceries for five hundred dollars a month, *if you'll leave me alone!*" There's not much worse than a husband who constantly jacks a wife around in the area of money. I remember thinking on many occasions, *I wish John would just let me settle into a budget before he goes changing it again.*

So remember this: God says of himself, "For every beast of the forest is Mine, the cattle on a thousand hills" (Psalm 50:10, NAS) and "Behold, to the Lord your God belong heaven and the highest heaven, the earth and all that is in it" (Deuteronomy 10:14, NAS). Not only does God own the cattle on a thousand hills, he also owns the hills. In fact, he owns all the dirt that exists. Yet, for a little while, you may have to treat your household income as if your husband owns it.

Becoming a Good Steward

Some women can just manage money. Many of us, however, struggle with this area of beauty. Whether we are addicted to shopping or the most frugal of buyers, there is always room for becoming a better steward.

The definition of a steward(ship) is: one employed in a large household to manage domestic concerns; an individual's responsibility to manage his life and property with proper regards to the rights of others. You are employed in the household of God to take care of his property, whether it's people, money, home, church, etc. You are commissioned by God to manage his estate.

Woman Beautiful is to manage her life and property, entrusted to her by God, with regards to his rights, not her personal desires or whims.

As difficult as it may be, we are to learn how to manage money, our homes, and our families in a way that pleases God. If we take a job outside of the home, then we are to manage that in regards to God's rights also. God owns it all; therefore, we're to manage "all" in regards to him—his desires, expectations, and purposes. Money and family seem to be the two most difficult areas of good stewardship that Woman Beautiful encounters; these are the two most important to us, and the wicked one knows it. Fully rely on God in these two areas. He loves your family more than you do, and he wants to bless you monetarily in order that you can give to his kingdom purposes, care for your family, and enjoy this life more fully.

Wise Spending

An easy way to help "generate" money for your household is to not spend it foolishly. Simple things like bargain shopping, making a grocery list and sticking to it, and shopping for needs rather than wants will be the same as working a job that pays. Cutting back on "self indulgences" like eating out, getting a daily soda pop or latté, and getting your hair cut or colored a little less frequently will save you money. Other money saving ideas include: checking out secondhand stores for furniture, clothing, lawn equipment, and household appliances; buying used rather than new cars; taking the time to make a weekly menu; eating out as an occasional treat, not as a lack of organization and planning; and saying *no* to whim purchasing—that goes for the kids too. It's mind-boggling when we take a good look at the way we spend money; so much of it could be spent more wisely. My sister, Teresa, and her husband, Brett, are faithful tithers and extreme givers and they save well, but Teresa is convinced that they could still be better stewards. Rightfully so. Good stewardship is not summed up in how much you give and how much you save; it is measured by how well you manage *all of it.* This valuable lesson is one my sister and I, along with our other siblings, were never taught; and we have struggled with trying to learn as adults. I regularly remind myself that "It *all* belongs to God!" I am simply the manager.

Sadly, many of you were never taught either. Not because you had bad parents but, like my parents, they too were never taught; you can only pass on what you know. It is time for you Woman Beautiful, to be in the know!

Beloved, be the victim no more in the area of your finances. Start the process of becoming a wise and faithful steward of all that God has entrusted to you. You are Woman Beautiful!

Teach me your ways, Holy God, that I will bring glory to you. I believe that you own it all and that I am merely your steward. Give me wisdom in giving, saving, and using your wealth. Where my husband and I don't agree, give me peace and change our hearts and minds accordingly. I trust you. Be glorified through my tithes and my offerings. Be glorified in my stewardship. In Jesus' name, I pray. Amen.

Beauty Tips

1. Ask yourself: Do you really believe all that you have belongs to God?
2. Make a commitment to get out of and stay out of debt.
3. Change your spending habits; quit spending what's leftover just because it's there.
4. Ask yourself these questions before spending:
    - Do I really need it?
    - Can I pay cash for it?
    - Will it glorify God?
5. Tithe faithfully and make offerings out of the money you have charge over.
6. Act wisely: look for sales, clip coupons, eat leftovers, make eating out an occasional opportunity, color your own hair; be creative in generating household income.
7. Save money in order to: help others, pay for emergency expenses, enjoy life without creating debt, and make offerings as God leads you to.
8. Grow money for future living, giving and spending without having to lower your *standard of living* in the future.

Sexual Beauty

"She shops wisely for her dress, pleasing to her husband yet appropriate" (Proverbs 31:22) (my paraphrase).

"The heart of her husband trusts her, he will have no lack of gain. She does him good and not evil all the days of his life" (Proverbs 31:11–12, NAS).

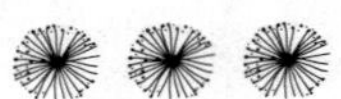

Step Six

Learn to Enjoy the Gift of Sexual Intimacy with Your Husband

Bedroom fellowship is one of my favorite topics of discussion. The world is very verbal about sex, mostly in an unhealthy and sinful way. Yet the local church still keeps it a pretty hush-hush subject. I told a friend once, "If I can pray about sex, I can pray about anything." You can too!

I have learned that one of the most powerful tools in my marriage is also one of the most pleasurable. Truly seek the Lord as you read this chapter. This may be your most difficult aspect of beauty, but I promise you, if you can trust God in this area of your marriage it will be an excellent time of sexual growth for you. Woman, you are *beautiful!*

> "There's a bigger picture and it doesn't just include me. Men are visual; it is important that I maintain my physical beauty as an expression of my love for my husband." Marlene Mains

For many women, this is the most difficult and not so enjoyable part of marriage. Childhood abuse, wrong teachings, and a seemingly insensitive husband make it very difficult for many women to enjoy sexual intimacy to its fullest. Yet, when we search the word of God, we find out that the act of lovemaking is a beautiful gift designed and given by God and that it has multiple purposes:

1. It keeps the oneness door open.
2. It stimulates communication.
3. It blesses your husband.
4. It blesses you. (It makes you happy by relieving emotional tension.) (Please notice I said it removes the tension that emotional stress causes—it does not remove the problem.)
5. It's good for your heart, both emotionally and physically. (Your husband's too!)
6. It keeps the husband and wife relationship strong.
7. It enlarges your family.
8. It tells your husband you value him and enjoy him.
9. It satisfies sensual desires.
10. It confirms God's interaction in your marriage.

Sex vs. Respect

After respect (the number one need of a man), sexual fulfillment is his next greatest need. It may seem to you that sex is his number one need. That is true for only a few men, and those men are out of balance relationally, namely with God. Even though most women could easily get by with engaging in sexual intimacy once a month,

men prefer to engage in this oneness more frequently. For her, sex has less to do with physical desire and more to do with responding to her husband's love and concern for her and their family. When he loves her well, sexual intimacy is a natural response to that love.

No Sex Tonight!

Unfortunately, many women deprive their husbands of sexual intimacy. They treat sex as a means of control rather than a pleasurable gift designed to bless the marriage relationship. If you are depriving your husband sexually, you are putting him in a place of compromise as well as temptation. He compromises because he has to "give in" to your control in order to "get some," and giving in demeans his manhood. Every case that I have seen where the wife uses sex as a means of control has been detrimental to the particular circumstance she wants to control and inevitably has become hazardous to the overall relationship. Sexual intimacy is a very strong desire of most all men; if that desire/need is not met regularly, the thought of an affair will be easily entertained and temptation will move from emotional flirting with another woman to physical intimacy with her.

Oneness

Much of the reading to follow is an excerpt from my book, *"Sex, Submission, and Spirituality: the Things Men Really Need to Know."* Some alterations have been made to minister to Woman Beautiful. Please keep in mind that I am writing to men about women as you read.

Too many times, I've heard men say, "Never are a husband and wife more one than when they are making love." This is a *stretched* exaggeration of the truth. In fact, I have only heard men say it. I have never once heard a woman confess, "My husband and I are never more one than when we are making love."

Remember what I said in the Relational Beauty segment, "Women have for a long time understood the oneness concept, and our oneness connection far surpasses a twenty-minute rendezvous once or twice a week. We have not successfully conveyed our understanding to man, nonetheless we know that true oneness far exceeds any kind of physical encounter we may share with the man we love. Please don't misunderstand, the sexual relationship is vital and evidence of a healthy and thriving marriage, but the marriage can be healthy and thriving no matter how often sex takes place. True oneness manifests when there is genuine love, respect, and honor in a marriage."

When the word of God expresses the "becoming one factor" in the book of Genesis, there is no reference to sex. As a matter of fact, Adam had expressed woman's value as being made from part of him and therefore he, man, being very attached to his mother and father would indeed have to leave their comfort and care, which was not sexual, and cleave to his wife, becoming one with her, separate from his parents.

> The man said, "This is now bone of my bones, and flesh of my flesh; She shall be called Woman,

> because she was taken out of Man." For this reason a man shall leave his father and mother, and be joined to his wife; and they shall become one flesh. And the man and his wife were both naked and were not ashamed.
>
> Genesis 2:23–25 (NAS)

Quite frankly, most women become somewhat frustrated when man tells us that we are never more one with him then when we are having sex. Many women feel somewhat manipulated and even devalued when they hear this. For Woman Beautiful, oneness is spiritual, emotional, and then physical. It is mutual value and respect. It looks like kindness, unconditional love, and acceptance. For her, good bedroom fellowship is a direct result of a healthy, love-filled relationship that is bathed in oneness through every circumstance of married life.

Because so much of her identity is found in her husband, it is impossible for her to separate herself from him. When he acts cold or uncaring, if his love seems to be here today but gone tomorrow, or if he says one thing then does another, she cannot see oneness in everyday circumstances. If he expresses unimportance in what concerns her, be it her home, children, goals, parents, God, or anything else of value to her, she experiences a oneness separation. When that oneness is inconsistent, her bedroom response will be inconsistent if her desire to engage in sexual intimacy exists at all.

Many women have experienced emotional abuse, neglect, rejection, and ridicule because of their bedroom performance. To tell her that complete oneness is never more powerful than when she is engaged in sex pushes her away from sexual intimacy rather than causing her to want to engage in it more often. Sexual oneness is temporal, and for her true oneness is more evident and more powerful in the "constant" of everyday-all-day-living, the kind of oneness rich in grace, reward, and lasting commitment toward her and her family.

Becoming one should have started long before the man and woman came together in the marriage bed. If we'd all done things the way the "Beloved and Lover" did them in the Song of Songs, we would have experienced oneness long before we lay upon the marriage bed. Like the famous lover, we women would have been ripe with love, ready to burst forth with passion fruit of plenty and our beloveds would have become students of us, knowing how to keep the love juices flowing, and *we would stay in those positions.* Yet, few couples experience this magnitude of oneness. After all, King Solomon himself admitted to having plenty of concubines to meet his sensual desires. Even the wisest fail to recognize that oneness starts with and is maintained in the spiritual realm.

God, the Key Ingredient to True Oneness

God created sex for the *married* man and woman; he was and is directly involved in the sexual relationship. To try to remove him from our lovemaking is like trying to remove vanilla from the vanilla bean. It can be done but the vanilla flavor is so much better if the entire bean is ground and then added directly to ice cream, baked goods,

or coffee. His desire for husband and wife is to partake of sexual intimacy often and to enjoy lovemaking at its most flavorful best.

My friend, Paula, once told me, "God will rock the house when you and your husband pray together." I knew she meant a spiritual, emotional, and sexual rocking just by the way she said the words. For the married Christian woman, spiritual intimacy with her husband is a type of unexplainable foreplay that moves her to say and respond, "Oh yeah, this is the man I desire. I will enjoy him often and to the fullest."

Inviting God into the bedroom is a natural occurrence for a husband and wife who love the Lord and are committed to him. Praying at mealtime, in the morning, and when someone is in need is good, but praying together at the end of the day is a nightcap that can, and regularly should, ignite a flame of passion that will not be extinguished until mutual sexual climax has been reached. A heart, mind, and life wholly committed to Christ is irresistible. The man (or woman) totally sold out to God is as a magnet, and bedroom fellowship is at its best when husband and wife have settled in their hearts, minds, and marriage to honor God in every area of their marriage, including their lovemaking.

What about Aggressive Sex?

I know many men would like for every other sexual encounter to be wild and passionate. Perhaps inviting God into the bedroom inhibits him from being the aggressive sex god he wants to be. It should not. God designed the act of lovemaking and intends for man and wife to experience it and enjoy it in its fullness. Therefore, lovemaking within marriage is almost boundary free.

When mutually agreed upon, the sex boundary is limited only to the four walls in which the marriage bed lies: as long as the sexual relationship does not cross the line from being accepted and permissive by God to perverse and sinful. When such things as having an affair, partner swapping, bringing in a third party to participate, having your children watch, or other such perverted behaviors occur, you can rest assured that you have overstepped the intent of God's wonderful and amazing gift. Even though variety is the spice of life, one cannot cross the line of perversion.

Although many women struggle with the concept of variety, it is an obstacle that can be overcome. Woman Beautiful has to allow her husband access to her heart and mind to find out what exactly prevents her from sharing in the "icing" of marriage with joy and pleasure. There is a reason why Woman Beautiful doesn't want to partake of wild passionate sex three times a week: perhaps she was seriously assaulted as a child or teenager; maybe Dad violated her while growing up; maybe Mom's many boyfriends had their way with her and now the slightest touch stirs up a sick feeling in her stomach; perhaps her husband wants to dive right in rather than taking the time to get to know her as a woman. Does she think that sex seems to be the only thing that draws her into her husband's thoughts?

Helping him discover what feels and sounds good to you and what doesn't will be well worth the time, frustration, and for many, the pain it takes you. Determine what you consider perverse, and then with that understanding patiently introduce new ideas into the lovemaking encounter.

Sensuality

When Woman Beautiful understands the senses, she realizes that anything can be sensual. The five senses are seeing, hearing, smelling, tasting, and touching. So, let's take hold of the true understanding of sensual: anything appealing to the senses. Food, for instance, is sensual in sight, smell, taste, and sometimes sound and touch. That's what makes it so pleasurable to eat. The act of lovemaking appeals to every one of the senses. To try to ignore one sense is to deprive the sexual encounter of a vital part of the total experience. It is important, while planning your lovemaking sessions, that you give attention to all five senses. This tells your husband that you are highly interested and involved in the sexual aspect of your marriage.

Hearing. Men have a unique way of tuning out anything they don't want to hear. Women, on the other hand, don't do that quite so easily. We've heard it said that during lovemaking women keep one ear in the hall waiting to hear a child who's awakened or the doorbell ring. Every creak and crack seems to catch her attention. When an unexpected noise occurs her concentration in the bedroom goes out the window and orgasm, though she may have been close, is now just as far away as it was twenty minutes earlier. She has to train herself, with her husband's help, to "tune out" anything not involved in the lovemaking chamber.

As you concentrate on what's ahead, ask your husband to help you settle the house for the evening. This help includes such things as getting the kids ready for and putting them to bed and making sure the doors are locked and that the lights and television have been turned off, as well as many others.

Seeing. There's a biblical wrong that has been taught by *many* counselors both Christian and non-Christian that really needs to be addressed here. Countless times I've heard it said, by both men and women, that God made man visual. Many unapologetically explain that God made man visual and that's just the way he is. Nothing can be done about it. The truth is, God created man, Adam, to look at Eve, his wife and say, "Wow! She is my desire, she is exciting, she is beautiful, and I want her." He was not created to look at any woman that walks by and say, "Ooh la la, she looks sexy. I'm gonna go home and have sex with my wife." What an insult to Holy God. We have perverted the exciting and amazing sexual relationship God designed as sacred for man and wife, and now have the audacity to blame it on the way God made the man. It is time for man (and woman) to acknowledge the way his Creator designed him, understand the fall and its effects, and respond accordingly.

God did design man to have a desire for his wife created by her physical appearance but to have those same

sexual desires created by looking at another woman is lust at best. Man has the responsibility to control his eyes and his thoughts. You've heard it said that the first look doesn't hurt, it's the second look that gets you in trouble. There is a lot to that little statement. We all notice the appearance of others, but when we look and *look* again then it's time to take charge of our behavior.

A word to those Woman Beautifuls growing in wisdom: I've heard it said, "It doesn't matter where my husband gets his appetite, as long as he comes home to eat." Woman Beautiful, if you have confessed this, rebuke that confession in the name of Jesus. It does matter where he gets his appetite! Lust in the heart of your husband is the same as the actual act of sex with that woman and that, Woman Beautiful,—fornication and adultery—grieves the heart of God. Every time your husband looks at a woman so intently that it causes him to want to have sex, it places unnecessary burden on your marriage—that of desiring the act of sex rather than the reward of a marriage relationship well managed. You have the difficult responsibility to address any of your husband's inappropriate or indulgent interaction with someone other than you.

Women are also guilty of taking that second look. We too need to take charge of our eyes and thoughts. When we look at our husbands, we should see the things of God that make him so attractive that no other man could turn our heads. If you can't see those things, ask God to open your eyes to let you see him the way God sees him. On those days that you know you and your husband will be engaging in bedroom fellowship, be in prayer that day that

God will enable you to look at him with eyes of tender connectedness; ask him to cover past hurts with the blood of Christ that those issues will not stand in the way of sweet communion between you and your husband. Finally, set your sights on the Lord; if you can't see your husband's need for this oneness, you should allow God to sustain you until at last you can and do respond to him with joy and total abandonment of everything that once kept you from enjoying your husband fully.

Now, with all that said, Dr. James Dobson once spoke tenderly about seeing his wife in a clingy nightgown and how that was all it took. Man is and should be aroused by his wife's physical beauty. Woman Beautiful, be deliberate in your physical attractiveness not for others, not just for yourself, but also for your husband. There are those nights when a sexual encounter should be the intent of a clingy nightgown.

Remember, respect and sex are very closely related in your husband's mind and emotion. As he sees your bedroom attractiveness extended toward him, he will know that he is respected and desired by you.

Taste. Both fresh breath and a clean body add to the flavorful taste of lovemaking. John and I have a simple understanding. If I say, "I'm going to brush my teeth and go to bed," then an invitation to a sexual encounter has been extended. Announcing a teeth brushing is not the only method of invite, but it is a clear one at our house. One thing for sure, if John comes to bed sucking on a cigarette, I know he's not desiring a roll in the sheets. Whether it's tobacco, alcohol, or bad breath, no one enjoys

an intimate face-to-face encounter as much as she could were his breath, and hers, fresh and clean. For women, bad breath is a real hindrance to being able to concentrate. I know it sounds petty, but you all know what I mean. We women have enough distractions while engaged in bedroom fellowship, bad breath in either mouth need not be another one.

Any body part that is kissed will have some kind of flavor. The taste of clean, fruit, or chocolate is always good. As noted in the physical section of *Woman Beautiful,* I suggest that you bathe or shower at least every other day. Most sexual encounters do not happen night after night, but they will on occasion. And if you're one of the many women who struggle with regular bathing, be sure to plan ahead so that some type of hygiene can be administered.

Smell. It would be unrealistic of me to say every sexual encounter needed to happen with two clean bodies. In fact, John knows when he has just the right amount of armpit body odor because I tell him. I heard it said once that if a woman has had a bad day with lots of stress, she should smell her husband's armpits and get soothing relief. I believe it! Who needs to have sex! Sometimes we women just need a good whiff of our husband's armpit!

There is a big difference between nasty, stinky, dirty, and natural body odor. God, in his infinite wisdom, knew that the natural body scents we put off would be an enhancement in lovemaking. Learn to take advantage of the natural scents each of your bodies produce. You will be amazed at what God foreknew about our gift of lovemaking. Cologne is wonderful to smell, but when you taste it, a bitter flavor overrides the delicious fragrance that it possesses. And there enters in one more distraction to the fellowship. Buy your husband a fragrance free body wash and ask him to skip the cologne so you can just smell him. You will be surprised at how yummy clean skin can be.

If you want to add fragrance, add it in the form of pillow and sheet sprays, candles, and room sprays. You can also add scents in the form of flavored body oils, lip balms, and glosses.

Touch. This is probably the most misunderstood aspect of the senses, especially in the area of sex. We women are quite finicky about the way we are touched: Not too fast, not too slow, not too hard, and not right there! As mentioned earlier, you should become a student of one another in an effort to understand each other sexually. Touch is eighty percent of lovemaking. If you're not getting touched in ways that are pleasing to you, then it is your responsibility to convey that to your husband.

Touch is everything to Woman Beautiful. Too much of a good thing can quickly become a bad thing. It would bring you great reward if you would teach your husband how to touch you in a way that pleases you. Don't be offended if he doesn't absolutely love something you think feels good. Lovemaking is give and get. When Woman Beautiful gets what pleases her, it becomes easy to give what is pleasing to her husband; more often than not, it is a positive sexual response. Don't continue to assume that he knows what you like in sexual intimacy. He only knows to do what he "thinks" should feel good to you. That doesn't make what he does to you wrong; it may only mean that it is not as effective as it could be.

Of course, spontaneous sexual encounters will be what you see, smell, taste, feel, and hear is what you get. Those spontaneous sexual encounters can be some of your most passionate lovemaking sessions. Don't get caught up in the realm of perfectionism; be willing to express love and desire for one another anytime, anyplace, and any way. Your husband will be wowed by your spontaneity.

Orgasm—Not As Easy As It Sounds

Most women struggle with having one orgasm per lovemaking encounter, let alone multiple orgasms. Under the right heart attitude, she could effortlessly have two, three, even four very good orgasms. Although very uncommon, when a woman is consumed by his love, when she trusts her husband, and when they are connected spiritually, uncontrolled, effortless peaks of pleasure can be expected from her during lovemaking. For her, orgasm is not the goal but the natural response to a man who loves her well. Perhaps that is one of the reasons God commanded man to love his wife in Ephesians 5:28. Not so much for her but that man could know he's doing his job well by her sexual response. Perhaps that response should be a clear "love gage" that keeps him on track: his Woman Beautiful's sexual pleasure is the natural response to his selfless love, respect, and adoration.

The rewarding fulfillment of every sexual encounter depends on your emotional and spiritual state. For Woman

Beautiful, sex is the icing on a well-baked cake, one with all the right ingredients and perfect baking time. We've heard that sex starts in the kitchen. This is not the baking I'm talking about. Good sex starts by mixing together the pure ingredients of love, acceptance, understanding, honor, trust, kindness, and gentleness, and then baking it in the fire of life without burning it. I know it sounds like a lot of work, but the husband and wife reward will be rich in the bedroom. The end result is a husband who knows he pleases his wife and a woman who wants to partake of him regularly.

Woman Beautiful and Regular Pleasurable Sex

Many a man fools himself into believing that his wife is all about sex simply because she understands how important sex is to her husband. A woman who wants to please her husband will learn how to cultivate that area of her marriage—not because she loves sex, but because she loves her man. In most relationships, the belief men have about this could not be further from the truth. Just because a woman flirts, touches, and even instigates sexual intimacy doesn't mean it's always on her mind; it simply means her husband is always on her mind and pleasing him is top priority.

Woman Beautiful's attempt to be pleasing to her husband should be bathed in prayer and adorned with a "no holds barred" attitude that frees her of his expectations. I know that you want more than just about anything to express your love for your husband in such a way that

conveys complete adoration toward him. Let go of his expectations of "how you should be in bed" and let Holy God grace you with peace and pleasure in understanding yourself and your husband in this vital area of your relationship.

I don't know how many women have said to me, "I can't even get close to him because he thinks I want to have sex; if I do one special sexual thing for him, he thinks it's an open invitation to do something every night." Just because Woman Beautiful wants to express her love for her husband by pleasing him sexually doesn't mean that's what she needs or wants on an every night basis. In fact, women only "need" to have sex once a month. That one time is right around ovulation. How creative was God to build in a hormonal stimulant at the time prime for conception. Every one of you can probably recognize that time of the month. You are extra flirty and assertive. You probably feel a little bit aroused and you will also be more likely to be offended it you don't reach orgasm during this session of lovemaking. A soothing and refreshing release comes from having an orgasm and there's not too much more frustrating for a woman than needing to have a good one and not getting there.

Right Mind, Right Heart

Although sexual intimacy is a vital part of your marriage relationship, it is not the most important part. Mutual love and respect far surpasses the sexual encounter. Most women possess the desire to be assertive in the bedroom, yet it becomes difficult when her husband seems to be indifferent, self-centered, or demanding. Quite frankly, such an attitude takes all of the fun out of lovemaking—as all Woman Beautifuls know. The word of God says, "... And yet her desire will be for her husband ..." (Genesis 3:16, NAS). This particular passage talks about her desire for him sexually. It is a natural desire that woman has for her husband, yes it is a sexual desire, but when that aspect of her marriage is dealt with carelessly, she will harness that desire until it becomes nonexistent. Beloved Woman Beautiful, you have to guard your bedroom fellowship attitude. It has to be about pleasing him—giving, and relying on God—getting. When you give to your husband what he needs, rest assured that you *will* get from God what you need.

Few men realize how detrimental their attitude toward the things that concern their wives can be. Woman Beautiful, if you can't convey to your husband just how hurtful his attitude is, then you have to forgive it, overcome your hurt, and give yourself freely to him, letting God give you the peace and desire to partake of this gift no matter how your husband views your lovemaking.

Let me offer you this advice: pray about your sexual beauty. And, if you have to, pray through your sexual encounters.

What about Sex Outside of Marriage?

God did not tell us to abstain from sex before marriage to be mean. His desire for his children is holiness and good

health. When you contaminate your body with sex outside of marriage, you contaminate the dwelling place of Holy God. You assault the Holy Spirit who is in you. His best is a temple that is sacred and holy, one that is set apart for his good purpose, a temple that is pure. Woman Beautiful, having sex outside of marriage exposes oneself to STDs; many of which are non-curable and can cause ill effects on her lifelong mate as well as her future unborn children. It also "marries" you to the person in which you have casual sex. When God gave Eve to Adam, the only ceremonial words he used were "be fruitful and multiply" (Genesis 1:26–28, NAS). The first marriage ceremony was conducted between God and the man and woman, and it was the act of sexual lovemaking. Each time a woman (or man) has sex with a different partner, they give themselves to the other person in a marriage covenant. It is no wonder our society is a mess. Each time a body is given away, a heart, or at least a piece of it, is given away also.

Woman Beautiful, if you have chosen a life of being unmarried, then you have chosen a life of abstinence. Read what the apostle Paul wrote about being single.

> Now concerning the things about which you wrote, it is good for a man not to touch a woman. But because of immoralities, each man is to have his own wife, and each woman is to have her own husband. The husband must fulfill his duty to his wife, and likewise also the wife to her husband. *(Paul is talking about sex here.)*
>
> The wife does not have authority over her own body, but the husband does; and likewise

> also the husband does not have authority over his own body, but the wife does. Stop depriving one another *(of sexual intimacy)* except by agreement for a time, so that you may devote yourselves to prayer, and come together again so that Satan will not tempt you because of your lack of self-control. But this I say by way of concession *(as a right of privilege of your husband's),* not of command. Yet I wish that all men were even as I myself am, *(single, being accountable only to God)* however, each man has his own gift from God, one in this manner, and another in that.
>
> 1 Corinthians 7:1–7 (NAS)
> (My paraphrase added).

Read that last line again. What an awesome truth! Abstinence and single-hood is a *gift* from God. Not all Woman Beautifuls are called to marriage. If you are that woman, delight in your gift of being single and commit yourself to serving the Lord. Enjoy the position that God has given you and become content with being as Paul was: able to serve the Lord in regards to no one but God alone. Woman Beautiful, if you can be content to live a life of abstinence, allowing the holy one of Israel to be your husband, you are a beautiful woman indeed!

Prayer for the Woman Beautiful who is married:

Father, you are my strength and my song. You have become my salvation.

Forgive the times that I have displayed inappropriate and even sinful sexual behavior. I am your child, you are my God;

teach my husband and me how to communicate our love for each other, to each other, in a beautiful and meaningful physical way. Enable me to confess to myself and to you those things that have prevented me from loving my husband freely. Lord, show him, through our bedroom fellowship, that I have utmost respect for him and that I truly desire him. Father, be glorified. In Jesus' holy name, I pray. Amen.

Prayer for the Woman Beautiful who is single:

Father, you alone are all that I need. Help me to see being single as the gift from you that it is. Consume me with yourself that I will be content in our relationship. If I am to marry, then so be it. Keep me pure until my wedding night. If I am not, then give me peace and joy that surpasses all understanding. Lord, strengthen me to be sexually pure. I understand that because I'm not married, I have been called to a life of abstinence. Lord, draw me close to you, guard my heart and my thoughts. Lead me in a life of purity and, Father, be glorified through me. I want to know and believe Isaiah 54:5 *that says, "For your Maker is your Husband, the Lord almighty is His name; the Holy One of Israel is your Redeemer; He is called God of all the earth" (*NIV*). Lord, I trust you to be my companion: the one who takes care of me and meets my every need. In Jesus' name, I pray. Amen.*

Beauty Tips

1. Ask God's forgiveness and repent for the way you may have inappropriately managed sex in your marriage.
2. Take the initiative to engage in bedroom fellowship at least once a week.

3. Read the necessary chapters in Ed and Gaye Wheat's book *Intended for Pleasure.*
4. Talk to your husband about the sexual concerns you have.
5. Seek wise counsel from a reputable Christian, and preferably a female counselor for any abuse you may have endured in the past or may be enduring presently.
6. Ask God's forgiveness and repent for the way you may have inappropriately managed sex outside of marriage.
7. Treat your body with respect to the Lord; it is his dwelling place.
8. Pray over your sexual relation with your husband.
9. Ask your husband's forgiveness for the times you've been unresponsive or have withheld physical intimacy from him.
10. Ask God for peace, pleasure, and prosperity in the sexual aspect of your marriage.
11. Thank God daily for the gift of being single.
12. Ask God to enable you to be sexually pure from this day forward.

Epilogue

> "Give her the product of her hands, and let her works praise her in the gates" (Proverbs 31:31, NAS).

As difficult as your walk of beauty may seem, it will be more than worth it. During those times when it appears as though you are failing, don't give up; instead, give in. Give in to the higher calling that God has for you, your family, your ministry, your career. Push on with an attitude of victory. Your purpose—no, your destiny is waiting on you; make the decision to become the best Woman Beautiful you can be. By applying the knowledge you now possess, you are destined to live a life that is rich in the blessings and promises of God, one that bears the fruit of godliness.

As you love him wholly and others in a more healthy way, you will leave behind a life that is riddled with hurt, confusion, and disappointment, trading it for a life that overflows with compassion toward others and one that is bathed in the understanding that your mental and emotional beauty are intertwined and that by taking every thought captive you can balance the mental and emotional in the power of Christ; you've not walked in the shoes of others and can therefore love them more completely, accept them more readily, and befriend them more selflessly. God created you to worship him and have fellowship with him, and with your sincere desire to possess more of him and less of yourself, he will fill you with his Holy Spirit in a way that you have never experienced before; physical beauty is purposed for good health in order that you can live out the destiny God created you for. God intends to trust you with wealth in order that his kingdom purposes would be advanced through you and that you would delight in your time on this earth; and sex is a gift from God for you and your husband to partake of regularly with mutual joy and pleasure.

You are loosed to enjoy life, to love and accept others just the way they are, and to bask in the glory of Holy God. His plan for you is bigger than you could ever hope or imagine. So, as you have already embarked on the greatest journey of your life and as the weeks, months, and years go by, look at the product of your hands because it alone will praise you!

> "I will never be the victim again. I am the *victor!*"
> Marlene Mains

> "The king is enthralled by your beauty; honor him for he is your lord" (Psalm 45:11, NIV).

Praying God's richest blessings on you always, you are *Woman Beautiful!*

Love in Christ ~ *Amanda*

Suggested "Must Reads"

- The Holy Bible
- *Boundaries: When to Say Yes, How to Say No, To Take Control of Your Life* by Dr. Henry Cloud and Dr. John Townsend
- *Love is a Decision: Proven Techniques to Keep Your Marriage Alive and Lively* by Gary Smalley and John Trent
- *The Power of Femininity: Discovering the Art of Being a Woman* by Michelle McKinney Hammond
- *The Total Woman: How to Make Your Marriage Come Alive!* by Marabel Morgan
- *The Power of a Praying Wife* by Stormie Omartian
- *Parenting Isn't for Cowards: The "You Can Do It" Guide for Hassled Parents from America's Best-Loved Family Advocate* Dr. James Dobson
- *Pray the Word: God Intended You to Win . . . Together* by Bob and LaRue McDaniel
- *The Power of a Praying Parent* by Stormie Omartian
- *Your Best Life Now: 7 Steps to Living at Your Full Potential* by Joel Olsteen
- *Six Hours One Friday* by Max Lucado
- *Lord Change Me!* by Evelyn Christianson

- *Ministering to the Lord: A Vision, A Search, A Discovery* by Roxanne Brant
- *The Maker's Diet: The 40 day health experience that will change your life forever* by Jordan S. Rubin
- *Your Money Counts: The Biblical Guide to Earning, Spending, Saving, Investing, Giving and Getting Out of Debt.* by Howard L. Dayton, Jr.
- *The Treasurer Principle: Discovering the Secret of Joyful Giving* by Randy Alcorn
- *Seedtime and Harvest* by Paula White
- *Intended for Pleasure: Sex Technique and Sexual Fulfillment in Christian Marriage* by Ed Wheat, M.D. and Gaye Wheat

Bibliography

Chapter 1: Mental and Emotional Beauty

- Joyce Meyer. Enjoying Everyday Life, daily broadcast. Trinity Broadcast Network. www.joycemeyer.org
- Juanita Bynum. Gospel Goes Classical, Disc 2: Tracks 3 and 4, Featuring Juanita Bynum & Jonathan Butler. Recorded live with the Gospel Goes Classical Symphony Orchestra and Choir, conducted by Dr. Henry Panion, III.

Chapter 2: Relational Beauty

- Michelle McKinney Hammond. *The Power of Femininity: Discovering the Art of Being a Woman.*
- Dr. James Dobson. *Focus On the Family* daily radiobroadcast. KJIL 99.1 Great Plains Christian Radio. 10:30 a.m. M-F www.kjil.com, www.focusonthefamily.com

Chapter 3: Spiritual Beauty

- Dr. Charles Stanley. *In Touch with Dr. Charles Stanley* daily radiobroadcast. KJIL 99.1 Great Plains Christian Radio. 10:00 a.m. M-F www.kjil.com, www.intouch.org
- Dr. Bill Bright. *Family Life Today* daily radiobroadcast. KJIL 99.1 Great Plains Christian

Radio. 11:00 a.m. M-F www.kjil.com, www.familylife.com

- Andrew Womack. *The Gospel Truth.* Trinity Broadcast Network (TBN) broadcast. www.awmi.com
- *Survival Kit for New Christians.* By Ralph W. Neighbour, Jr. and Bill Latham, LifeWay Press, Nashville, Tennessee

Chapter 4: Physical Beauty

- Jordan Rubin. *The Maker's Diet; The 40 day health experience that will change your life forever.*
- Kathy Troccoli. Heritage Keepers Women's Conference, Wichita, Kansas.

Chapter 5: Financial Beauty

- Dave Ramsey. Video series: *Financial Peace University.* Financial Peace Revised. Published in 2003 by Viking Penguin, a member of Penguin Putnam, Inc.